ISRAEL

AND THE

CHURCH

AMIR TSARFATI

HARVEST HOUSE PUBLISHERS
EUGENE, OREGON

Cover designed by Faceout Studio

Interior design by KUHN Design Group

Cover photo © sommthink, revers, Rich Carey, alfocome, Didecs / Shutterstock; tzahiv / Gettyimage

For bulk, special sales, or ministry purchases, please call 1-800-547-8979. Email: Customerservice@hhpbooks.com

M is a federally registered trademark of the Hawkins Children's LLC. Harvest House Publishers, Inc., is the exclusive licensee of the trademark.

Israel and the Church
Copyright © 2021 by Amir Tsarfati
Published by Harvest House Publishers
Eugene, Oregon 97408
www.harvesthousepublishers.com

ISBN 978-0-7369-8270-2 (pbk.)
ISBN 978-0-7369-8271-9 (eBook)
ISBN 978-0-7369-8448-5 (eAudio)

Library of Congress Cataloging-in-Publication Data

Names: Tsarfati, Amir, author.
Title: Israel and the Church / Amir Tsarfati.
Description: Eugene : Harvest House Publishers, [2021] | Summary: "In
   Israel and the Church, bestselling author and native Israeli Amir
   Tsarfati helps readers recognize the distinct contemporary and future
   roles of both the Jewish people and the church, and how together they
   reveal the character of God and His perfect plan of salvation"--
   Provided by publisher.
Identifiers: LCCN 2020045402 (print) | LCCN 2020045403 (ebook) | ISBN
   9780736982702 (trade paperback) | ISBN 9780736982719 (ebook)
Subjects: LCSH: Bible--Prophecies. | Israel (Christian theology)--Biblical
   teaching. | Church--Biblical teaching. | Bible. Revelation--Meditations.
Classification: LCC BS647.3 .T73 2021 (print) | LCC BS647.3 (ebook) | DDC
   236/.9--dc23
LC record available at https://lccn.loc.gov/2020045402
LC ebook record available at https://lccn.loc.gov/2020045403

Printed in the United States of America

21 22 23 24 25 26 27 28 / BP / 10 9 8 7 6 5 4 3 2 1

I dedicated my first two books to my family.
However, family can also extend beyond
just those you're related to.

I want to dedicate this book to the Behold Israel team,
ministry partners, and close friends. Like Aaron and Hur,
you have held my arms up through the good times and the bad.
I love you, and I am so thankful God has blessed me with you.

ACKNOWLEDGMENTS

First and foremost, I want to thank the Lord for His faithfulness throughout my life. Before I was even born, He loved me deeply and had a plan for my life. What a blessing it is to serve my Savior each and every day.

Steve Yohn, I want to thank you for your assistance in writing this book. When it looked like we were going to lose you during the writing process, prayers were offered up around the world—and God answered! Steve, I thank God for you and for all that He has done in you and through you these past months.

I want to thank my wife, Miriam, my four children, and my new daughter-in-law. Your love and support for me have never waned, even as the Lord has led me away from home so often. A husband and father could not be more blessed than I have been.

I want to thank my team at Behold Israel for their love, support, and dedication—Mike, H.T. and Tara, Gale and Florene, Donalee, Joanne, Nick and Tina, Jason, Abigail, Jeff, and Kayo. Also, thanks to all your spouses and children who often sacrifice their family time with you to further the spreading of God's Word.

Special thanks to the many translators who have made my YouTube messages available in 20 different languages. Also, I offer great thanks to the many ministry coordinators around the globe who ensure everything runs smoothly at our conferences.

Thank you, Shane, for your great work on our graphics and social media. Thank you, Jon, for our excellent app and website. Thank you, Don, for your excellent work at Veni Graphics. Also, thank you to the team at Tenfold BPO for all that you do.

Thank you to Barry Stagner, Jan Markell, and Rick Yohn for your wisdom and your rich insight into God's Word. Thank you also to Pastor Jack Hibbs and Pastor Steve Berger and your wonderful families.

Thank you to our many ministry friends, including Andy and Gail, Wayne and Cindy, and Amanda and Ian. Your wisdom, mentoring, and practical help are invaluable. This could not be done without you!

A shout-out to our Youth Adult Discipleship Group—it's been amazing to watch those of you in the next generation grow in your dedication to Christ. And for the three young couples who met during one of our tours and have since gotten married—mazel tov!

Thank you to Bob Hawkins and Steve Miller, and the wonderful team at Harvest House, for all your hard work in making this book happen.

Finally, thank you so much to the hundreds of thousands of followers, prayer partners, and ministry supporters of Behold Israel. This ministry would not exist without you.

CONTENTS

PART 1:

TWO CHOSEN PEOPLES

CHAPTER 1

FEAR NOT

An Unchanging God in
an Ever-Changing World

I t's Christmas Day, 2019. All twelve seats around the dining table are filled—two generations gathered together. In the living room are a couple smaller tables surrounded with children, the second table having been added this year due to the family expanding to a third generation. Every little hand and every small face appears to have some type of food on it—potatoes, gravy, butter, even corn has found a way to stick on the cheeks of several. Two of the moms excuse themselves from the main table to begin the process of wiping down children and collecting dishes.

Back at the main table, everyone pushes themselves back a little from the food to resist the temptation to indulge in the leftovers. That's when Uncle Barney speaks up—and everyone rolls their eyes. Barney has always been a bit of a conspiracy theorist and, whenever he's given the opportunity, is ready to share his views about the Kennedy assassination, the moon landings, and where Jimmy Hoffa is buried. Before Mom can rescue everyone with the offer of pie, Barney launches into his latest.

"Have you been watching the news?" he begins, using his traditional six-word intro. "Not the networks or cable junk, but the real news. I saw the other day that there are people in China getting sick from some new virus. People are saying this has the potential to explode across the world. It could even reach pandemic status. If that happens, it's possible that we may have to shut down the whole American economy. There could be mass quarantines and stay-at-home orders. Only essential businesses would be allowed to stay open. Pastors may even get arrested just for holding church services."

"Okay, Barney," Dad interrupts, "that's getting ridiculous. The idea of the entire national economy shutting down is silly enough, but pastors not allowed to hold services? Come on, we still have a Constitution."

This leads to a debate between Barney the kook and his outlandish pandemic theory and Dad the realist, whose faith is in the established rule of law. The volume of their banter rises as the tension level increases. Finally, when it seems the back-and-forth is about to blow, Mom rushes in carrying a cherry pie in one hand and an apple pie in the other. She asks Dad, "Honey, will you run into the kitchen? I seem to have forgotten my serving knife."

Crisis averted—another year when Mom saves the day.

If you had been at that dinner table, whose side would you have been on? I most definitely would have been on the "Let's have some pie" side. Instead of pie, however, Dad would have had to eat some crow when, a few months later, it become evident that for once, a crazy theory voiced by Barney turned out to be true. What seemed like an absurdity just a few months ago is now a bizarre reality.

As I am writing this, the coronavirus pandemic has swept the world. I am multiple weeks into a nationwide quarantine, and people are now beginning to talk about how we might be able to start opening the country again at an undetermined point in the future. This is a time unlike any other that this world has ever seen, where globally, billions of people have retreated into their homes by government mandate. Thus far, more than 200 countries are afflicted, and the number continues to grow.

By the time you read this, I expect that my nation, Israel, and the rest of the world will be well on the way to opening up. However, from where I sit right now, the question of our global future is still up in the air.

Unlike past incidents of world conflict, this enemy has chosen no ideology to align with. It has not gathered a coalition of nations to its side. It is not seeking to conquer new territory or to enslave other people groups. This is a lone enemy with one goal in mind—death. There is no reasoning with it. There is no capital city where one could send a peace envoy. This enemy is mindless, irrational, and very powerful. It is also microscopic, invisible to the naked eye, which makes developing a defense strategy against it very difficult.

This is not a battle that will bring about human extinction. There will not be a genocidal slaughter of people groups. The masses will not be forced to leave their homes to be sold off in a foreign land. If anything, this virus is causing people to stay locked inside of their homes. Eventually, I believe that we will track down this enemy and defeat it. We will find a way to treat it and vaccinate against it. We will overcome, as we have so many enemies in the past. But it will be a long battle. Again, as you read this now, I expect that the world will be well on its way to defeating this enemy.

However, in April 2020, as I write this chapter, the war wages. Fear has swept through nations and people groups. Even in the church there is worry over sickness and dying, as well as anxiety surrounding the more temporal concerns of collapsing economies and ongoing government-mandated moratoriums against meeting together. "Where is God in this?," people ask as they pray for a COVID-sick parent or spouse that they can't even visit.

FEAR NOT

Let's travel back to a time in history when the people of Israel were in grave danger. An enemy was coming—one that was not microscopic and didn't invade a person's body. Rather, this army was all too visible as they trampled through nation after nation, causing death and destruction with their swords and spears and other dangerous weapons of war.

Once this great war machine locked its eyes onto a prize, that city was sure to fall. Now, this nation's gaze had settled on Jerusalem.

The prophets had long said that from the north, evil would come. This particular northern evil had a name—Assyria. Decades earlier, this same empire had annihilated the kingdom of Israel—the ten tribes that, under King Jeroboam, had separated from the southern kingdom of Judah generations before. In 722 BC, the Assyrian king Shalmaneser V invaded his rebellious vassals and overtook the nation. The defeated population who had survived the bloody assault were relocated to a faraway land. Now Assyria was back, this time under King Sennacherib, and it was gunning for Judah.

Isaiah was a prophet in that time, and, as such, was acting as God's spokesman to His chosen people. He was married to a prophetess, and together they had two sons—both with quite unusual names. The eldest was named *Shear-Jashub*, which means "a remnant shall return." We meet the second son in Isaiah 8:3-4, when the prophet reports, "I went to the prophetess, and she conceived and bore a son. Then the LORD said to me, 'Call his name Maher-Shalal-Hash-Baz; for before the child shall have knowledge to cry "My father" and "My mother," the riches of Damascus and the spoil of Samaria will be taken away before the king of Assyria.'" This boy's mouthful of a name means "speed the spoil, hasten the booty."

While there may be a debate as to which would cause a child to get picked on more in school—that lengthy name or its meaning—it is actually a special moniker to bear. These progenies of prophets carry prophetic names that tell of the past and the future of Israel. *Maher-Shalal-Hash-Baz* points to Israel's past of being looted and robbed by an enemy that comes from the outside. *Shear-Jashub*, however, carries in his name a beautiful promise—the remnant will return to the land of Israel.

It is true that I am having to write this during a government-mandated lockdown—very likely an isolation you are familiar with. What is amazing in my case is that I am doing this in the land of Israel. After 2,000 years of being away from the long, narrow stretch of mountains and farmlands and streams and wilderness given to Abraham and his descendants, I am living proof that God's promises never fail. I am part of the remnant—a child of the tribe of Judah—living in the lush beauty of the Valley of Armageddon. I and all my fellow Jews in Israel are the embodiment of *Shear-Jashub*. How great is our God!

The Assyrian army was coming at Judah from the north. The people were frightened and looking for hope. Isaiah stood in front of the fearful crowd. He was to serve as God's conduit to give the listeners comfort and to remind them of His promises for a great future.

Isaiah began with an introduction to the ultimate Source of the words he was about to speak: "Thus says the LORD, who created you, O Jacob, and He who formed you, O Israel" (Isaiah 43:1). Right from the beginning, Isaiah's words were encouraging: "The God who made you is now speaking to you." Reminiscent of David's words in Psalm 139:13-16, his message said, "God knows you. He formed you. All your days were already written into the Lord's books before you were formed. You are not just some random nation. God is not speaking to an anonymous rabble. He is reaching out to His beloved creation."

Isaiah now spoke God's words to the listeners:

Fear not, for I have redeemed you;
I have called you by your name;
You are Mine.
When you pass through the waters, I will be with you;
And through the rivers, they shall not overflow you.
When you walk through the fire, you shall not be burned,
Nor shall the flame scorch you.
For I am the LORD your God,
The Holy One of Israel, your Savior (Isaiah 43:1-3).

Read those words again. Let them sink in. How do they make you feel? This is the character of God. These words are who He is. And this message is not just for the people of Israel, but for all who belong to Him. He is saying, "I am God. I am the Creator of the heavens and the earth. Yes, I am the God of My beloved nation, Israel, that I have set apart, but I am the Savior of the people of the church too."

I don't know where you are right now or what situation you are in.

I just know that you need to believe in the Creator of the world. While His name may be the God of Israel, He is your personal Savior. Why do I have such peace in the middle of the COVID-19 insanity? The same God who told Israel not to worry about the Assyrian army is the same God who comforts me today with His love and power. The same God who can destroy a great superpower can certainly eradicate a virus.

The Lord continues:

> I gave Egypt for your ransom,
> Ethiopia and Seba in your place.
> Since you were precious in My sight,
> You have been honored,
> And I have loved you;
> Therefore I will give men for you,
> And people for your life.
> Fear not, for I am with you;
> I will bring your descendants from the east,
> And gather you from the west;
> I will say to the north, "Give them up!"
> And to the south, "Do not keep them back!"
> Bring My sons from afar,
> And My daughters from the ends of the earth—
> Everyone who is called by My name,
> Whom I have created for My glory;
> I have formed him, yes, I have made him (Isaiah 43:3-7).

In those first seven beautiful verses of Isaiah 43 are the past, the present, and the future of Israel. And they contain His message of hope to "everyone who is called by My name," and that includes the church. His words are for all whom He has "created for [His] glory." That includes both the Jews who are His chosen nation, as well as all who believe in Him who are His beloved children. The message to all who will listen to Him is this: "When you feel alone, you are not. When you are afraid, remember that I am with you all the way. Even in the midst of the worst of situations, I am there."

We must understand the truth of God's presence in the midst of the imperfect times. God didn't create the imperfect. God doesn't cause the imperfect. But God works through the imperfect. That's who He is. He is a perfect God who carries out His perfect will in imperfect people who live in an imperfect world. When God first created this universe, everything was perfect. The perfect God established His perfect creation by His perfect Word. Then humanity expressed the free will with which the Lord had gifted it, and everything blew apart. Sin entered the world, and with sin came death. Creation was separated from Creator.

God didn't create the imperfect.
God doesn't cause the imperfect.
But God works through the imperfect.

A NEED FOR HOPE

Picture Adam and Eve exiting the Garden of Eden. Inside the Garden, everything was beautiful. Food was plentiful and the surroundings were lush. But most wonderful of all, God was there. Fellowship with the Creator was readily available, and they would walk with Him in the cool of the day. But when they walked out, all of that "perfect" was left behind. What an empty, tragic moment.

It wasn't only mankind that suffered in that inaugural act of humanity's sinful rebellion. Nature experienced its own death throes as well. At the bite of the fruit, all creation was cursed with death. Mankind was given both spiritual and physical death. Because nature has no spirit, it only faced the latter. Every creature that has ever existed in the animal kingdom—from mosquito to mammoth, from microbe to meerkat—has had an expiration date. For each, life began. For each, life ended.

However, it isn't just the organic that faces physical death. The inorganic, too, is dying. The mountains, rivers, and valleys were created perfectly. All natural systems and weather patterns and harvest cycles were established exactly as they should be. Then came sin, and with it, death—and the natural world has been on a downward slide ever since. Floods, tornadoes, earthquakes, and, yes, viruses are all part of the deterioration of God's perfect creation.

There is no hope for the natural world. It is in a hospice situation, and we are simply awaiting its final demise. No matter how many climate change protocols are established and how many fishing ships are pestered by Greenpeace, the decay and collapse of this world will not be halted. That doesn't mean we shouldn't take great care of our beautiful earth as stewards of God's creation. But there is a reason that when the end of time comes, God will establish new heavens and a new earth.

When it comes to humanity, however, there is hope. The natural world will be destroyed. In the words of pharaoh from Cecil B. DeMille's epic *The Ten Commandments*, "So let it be written, so let it be done." Destruction for you and me, though, has not been decreed and sealed. God has given us an opportunity to remove the death sentence of sin. The only effective solution for our sin problem is faith in Jesus Christ. He paid our penalty—He died our death on the cross.

When death is removed, what is left? Life. Jesus said, "I am the way, the truth, and the life. No one comes to the Father except through Me" (John 14:6). Another way to look at that verse is to say that Jesus is the way to the truth that gives us life. By believing in Him as our Savior and committing to Him as our Lord, we are, in a sense, readmitted into the Garden—that glorious place where we can once again have peace and fellowship with our creator God.

GOD'S LONG-SUFFERING GRACE

Let's go back to those wonderful words of Isaiah 43. Trouble was coming for the nation of Judah. But along with the trouble came hope. God will not judge or afflict His people without also telling them the way out of their mess. As we've just seen with His plan for removing sin and reconciling us to Himself, there are situations we will face that are too big for us to handle. But God will not leave us hanging help-lessly. There is always hope when we look to Him. And where we find hope, that is where we find true peace.

Israel, as a nation, was far from perfect. The people had a strong propensity for rebellion, idol worship, and ignoring the law of God. There are many Christians these days who will say that because of the nation's imperfection, God has discarded them. Jesus Christ came to the Jews, but they didn't want anything to do with Him. "He came to His own, and His own did not receive Him" (John 1:11). The Jews rejected Him; therefore, He now rejects them. That's it, case closed, the Jews have been kicked to the curb in favor of the church.

Imagine if these Christians were to apply that same logic to them-selves. Any sin is rebellion against God. How many acts of rebellion and rejection of God's lordship does it take to get booted out of the family? In the Garden, it took only one sin to separate us from God. I know I have plenty more than one sin to my credit since receiving Christ as my Savior. If sin can cause the Father to permanently reject His children, what percentage of the church could stand before God today?

But that's not the way He works, is it? A loving Father does not kick His children out of His family. He will bring hard times in order to discipline them. He will allow pain to straighten His people out. But the Lord who said that we should forgive not just seven times but "sev-enty times seven" (Matthew 18:22) does not put a credit limit on His mercy. Rather than see Israel's rebellion as a reason for God's rejection, we should see it as setting the stage for us to witness His glorious mercy. It is in the truth that God didn't reject a people as deserving of rejec-tion as Israel that we find hope that God will never reject a people so deserving of rejection as are we, His church. And it is in this constancy of His love and commitment to us that we can find peace in the midst of a coronavirus crisis or any other trial we face.

Does our "no-matter-what" security in the family of God mean that sin doesn't really matter? Do we now have a free ticket to live however we want? God promised the Israelites through Isaiah that because of their hypocritical hearts and empty worship, He was going to bring pain their way. Yet it would be the pain of discipline, not the destruction that accompanies judgment. God's long-suffering grace and patience are painted in beautiful colors when, in Isaiah 1, after an accusation of unfaithfulness and a declaration of the promised disciplinary suffering, the Lord says, "I will restore your judges as at the first, and your counselors as at the beginning. Afterward you shall be called the city of righteousness, the faithful city" (verse 26). Because of God's love, He will never cast away His own. The hand that disciplines is the same hand that restores. There are times when God will allow us to go through the storm, but He always does it for a reason and only for a time.

THE POWERFUL PRESENCE OF GOD

That disciplining, restoring hand is also the hand that protects. Let's go back to Isaiah 43 and the coming of the Assyrians. There, God talked to a frightened nation that was about to be attacked by the most terrible superpower of the time. He reminded them, "When you pass through the waters, I will be with you; and through the rivers, they shall not overflow you" (Isaiah 43:2).

"Wait, Amir, isn't this an army attacking by land? Why is God talking about waters?" The Lord was reminding the people of Israel what happened back in Exodus 14, when they walked through the waters of the Red Sea. The massive superpower army of that day—the Egyptians—was charioting behind the Israelites, trapping the helpless people between death by sword and death by drowning. But then God did a miraculous work, and the Hebrews enjoyed a dry hike to the other side.

By the way, there is an underwater land bridge between the two sides of the Red Sea connecting Egypt and Saudi Arabia. It is a geographical feature that no one can explain. On the shore at either side of the land bridge are places that once had columns—from the time of King Solomon—that marked where the crossing of the Red Sea took place. So when the children of Israel passed through, they didn't have to walk all the way to the bottom of a deep ocean and then back up. They went across a land bridge that was much higher than all the underwater terrain around it. Even before the Israelites knew they had a problem, God had led them to the exact place where He would solve that problem for them.

When the situation for the Egypt-fleeing Hebrews was at its worst, God was there. "The Angel of God, who went before the camp of Israel, moved and went behind them; and the pillar of cloud went from before them and stood behind them. So it came between the camp of the Egyptians and the camp of Israel" (Exodus 14:19-20). This "Angel of God" was a Christophany—a revelation of Christ in the Old Testament. In a time of trouble, the preincarnate Jesus was there protecting His people. That's how God operates, and He has proved His care for His people time after time.

When Israel was about to face the insurmountable walls of Jericho, the Lord appeared again—this time before Joshua.

> Joshua went to Him and said to Him, "Are You for us or for our adversaries?" So He said, "No, but as Commander of the army of the LORD I have now come." And Joshua fell on his face to the earth and worshiped, and said to Him, "What does my Lord say to His servant?" Then the Commander of the LORD's army said to Joshua, "Take your sandal off your foot, for the place where you stand is holy." And Joshua did so (Joshua 5:13-15).

Just like with Moses and the burning bush, the ground was holy because God was there. The presence of an angel doesn't make a place holy. It is the presence of God that sanctifies a location.

When Daniel's three friends, Shadrach, Meshach, and Abednego, were thrown into the fiery furnace, Christ was present with them:

> King Nebuchadnezzar was astonished; and he rose in haste and spoke, saying to his counselors, "Did we not cast three men bound into the midst of the fire?" They answered and said to the king, "True, O king." "Look!" he answered, "I see four men loose, walking in the midst of the fire; and they are not hurt, and the form of the fourth is like the Son of God" (Daniel 3:24-25).

Jesus was in the fire with those three brave young men. He was there when the Israelites crossed the river and came to Jericho. He was there when the camp crossed the Red Sea. He was there! This is the same Jesus who, more than two-and-a-half millennia ago, commanded Israel to return to their land and is smoothing the path today as they continue to arrive.

This is the same Jesus who is now commanding you, wherever you live, "Fear not, for I am with you." This is the promise of Psalm 23:4: "Yea, though I walk through the valley of the shadow of death, I will fear no evil; for You are with me; Your rod and Your staff, they comfort me." This is the hope found in Isaiah 35:4: "Say to those who are fearful-hearted, 'Be strong, do not fear! Behold, your God will come with vengeance, with the recompense of God; He will come and save you.'" God is with you. He is watching His people—in Israel and in the church.

There is no reason for us to fear what we see happening around us. Paul wrote, "God has not given us a spirit of fear, but of power and of love and of a sound mind" (2 Timothy 1:7). Those three—power, love, and a sound mind—must come together for us to have true peace. We cannot overcome fear without the power of God. However, if we are not expressing His love to others, He may withhold His power in discipline. If we don't have a sound mind and are doubting God's truth and character, then we likely won't turn to Him in our times of trouble. All three of those characteristics must be present in our lives for us to live with a God-given fearlessness.

A PROVEN FAITHFULNESS

I am in the middle of Israel, and it is peaceful here. Yet Israel is one of the most threatened countries on planet Earth. There is no other nation whose neighbors so openly vow to make it extinct. Amazingly, the rest of the world is okay with that. Even from the podium of the UN General Council, world leaders call for the destruction of Israel. Still, here I am, not only personally experiencing the peace of God, but looking at evidences of God's peace all around me. What is the coronavirus to God? Nothing. If you choose to fear rather than to trust Him who says, "Fear not," then where is your faith?

God is faithful—a character quality He has demonstrated through this beautiful land and through the people whom He has brought home. His proven faithfulness is not something that I can remain quiet about. This is why Behold Israel was born. Behold Israel—"Look at His Land"—is proof that God exists. This is the evidence that He is faithful to all His promises. The reason God left Israel to stand even after its history of failure and rebellion is to serve as a testimony to you to not be afraid. The same God who has been faithful to this oft-times beleaguered nation is also faithful to you who are in the church.

God said that from Jacob He would create a nation. Then, as He worked through Jacob's descendants, He said, "I will separate them. I will work through them. Through these rebellious people I will demonstrate My love; I will reveal My Word to the world; and I will bring My Son, the Messiah, to all mankind. And through this tiny nation I will prove that if you will humble yourself and pray and turn away from your wicked ways, I will forgive you. I will embrace you. I will call you My own."

God is not in the business of destruction and punishment. People bring those sorrows upon themselves. In 2 Thessalonians 2:10-11, Paul said that it is only after people have rejected the love of the truth that can save them that God gives them delusions. He didn't give them delusions so that they would reject the Word of God; He gave them delusions because they rejected the Word of God.

THE DAY OF SALVATION

God sent His only begotten Son to bring salvation to the world. This is the other side of the "God's chosen people" coin. The common belief among the Jews was that God worked only with Israel. But then Jesus came into the world. When the time was right, the Messiah headed down to the Jordan River. When He arrived, He found a Jewish priest named Johanon—"God will have mercy." This Johanon, or John, spotted Jesus and declared, "Behold! The Lamb of God who takes away the sin of the world!" (John 1:29). His words were not "of Israel," but "of the world."

This sacrificial Lamb of God is for you in Wuhan, China. It's for you in Seoul. It's for you in Singapore and Manila, in Tehran and Baghdad, in Ankara and Istanbul. Jesus died for you in Beirut and Damascus and Berlin and Frankfurt. He shed His blood for you in Paris, London, Barcelona, and Madrid—for you in Milan and Rome and Zagreb and Bucharest, in Budapest and Brussels and Amsterdam and Copenhagen. Salvation is available for you as a free gift in the United States from New York to Los Angeles, down south to Mexico City and São Paulo and Rio de Janeiro. Jesus is opening His arms to you in Auckland and Sydney and Melbourne and Perth, in Nairobi and Kampala, Lagos and Johannesburg.

When you open your heart to the love and forgiveness of Jesus Christ, He will make you a new person. He will spark a light in you—a light of new life, a light of eternity. Then He will use that light in you to shine His truth to the world. Jesus said in the Sermon on the Mount,

> You are the light of the world. A city that is set on a hill cannot be hidden. Nor do they light a lamp and put it under a basket, but on a lampstand, and it gives light to all who are in the house. Let your light so shine before men, that they may see your good works and glorify your Father in heaven (Matthew 5:14-16).

It is through your peace during crisis that those around you can discover God's peace. It is through your lack of fear that your friends and family members will be able to see that with God, there is no need to fear.

Has the light of God entered your life so that you can be the light of the world? Do you have the Holy Spirit in you—the oil in your lamp—so that you can shine out His hope? And if you have been born anew into eternal life, are you letting your light shine?

Before His crucifixion, Jesus encouraged His disciples with these words: "In the world you will have tribulation; but be of good cheer, I have overcome the world" (John 16:33). This coronavirus is just a tribulation of the world, as are all trials that befall you. Don't be afraid. Instead, be of good cheer, because Jesus has overcome the world.

It all comes down to our Savior. "God has given us eternal life, and this life is in His Son. He who has the Son has life; he who does not have the Son of God does not have life" (1 John 5:11-12).

Do you have the Son? Have you made Jesus your Savior and Lord? If not, today is the day of salvation. Why spend another day with questions filling your life? If you do have the Son, then rejoice. No matter what is going on around you—no matter what viruses may come your way—God is with you. And as He has done from the beginning of time, He will continue to care for His own—whether they are of the people of Israel or of the church, or, like me, of both.

CHAPTER 2

TWO TRUMPETS ARE BETTER THAN ONE

The Shared Purpose of Israel and the Church

The air was cooler now that the season had begun to change, but that didn't stop the sweat trickling down from where the man's son sat on his shoulders. He had lifted the boy to his perch to keep him from getting pulled away by the current of the crowd. Up on dad's shoulders was also the only likely way his son would be able to see anything. This was the first time that the boy had been old enough to make the week-long journey to Jerusalem for the festival. It would be a shame if his view of the event was limited to the dusty cloaks and grimy sandals that would have surrounded him.

The Temple courtyard continued to fill, and the bodies pressed tighter and tighter together. A murmur rushed through the crowd, and the eyes of father, son, and thousands of others looked up to the surrounding wall. Two Levites, spotlessly dressed in their ceremonial robes, had mounted the wall from opposite ends and were marching toward a meeting place at the center. Tucked under the right arm of each was a long, silver trumpet. With each step, the reflective glare from the sun against the shiny metal bounced across the crowd, leaving hundreds trying to blink away blue spots.

When the two trumpeters met, they turned away from the Temple toward the surrounding city and the land beyond. As one, they slowly raised the instruments to their lips, inhaled deeply, then blew. The note from each trumpet merged with its counterpart into one resounding blare. Even from behind the sound was piercing, and the man felt his son's hands lift to cover his small ears. The Levites stopped, and the sound echoed back from the Mount of Olives to the east. Then came a second blast, then a third. After the seventh blast, the Levites lowered their instruments and began their marches back to where they had begun. As they did, the people in the crowd lowered their heads in prayer.

In his ear, the man heard his young son whisper, "What now, Father?"

"Now there's a sacrifice."

"And then what?"

"And then we go home."

"Wait," the boy said, sounding confused and disappointed. "You mean that's it?"

"Well, there will probably be some singing and dancing. But, yes, that's it."

There was silence for a minute while the man prepared his heart for the sacrifice that was about to be offered on the great bronze altar. But he could sense his son trying to process the information he had been given, and he couldn't help but anticipate the next question that he knew would come. Sure enough, the boy asked, "If that's all there is, then why do we come? It hardly seems worth it."

"We come," the man replied, "because God said to come. Now hush for the offering."

INSTRUMENTS WITH A PURPOSE

In the Bible, the one instrument you read about most is the trumpet. You may find a harp or a lyre here, maybe a cymbal or a tambourine there, but, if you were a musician looking for job security, you would have wanted to start those trumpet lessons early. Today, when people think of trumpets, they picture a series of brass tubes with three valves, with a mouthpiece at one end and a flared bell at the other. But most of the trumpets found in the Bible are more organic in nature. Typically, the Old Testament trumpet refers to a *shofar*, which is a hollowed-out ram's horn. The tip of the horn is cut off to create a small hole for someone to, as the great actress Lauren Bacall said to Humphrey Bogart, "put your lips together and blow."

One of the more cringeworthy moments I often experience when I am leading tours of Israel is when people discover the shofars that are for sale in many of the gift shops. I will watch as a group gathers together. One man (typically, it's men who do this) will pick up a ram's horn, bring it to his lips, then blow. The sound that comes out is usually reminiscent of the last sound the ram probably made before it lost its horns.

But that is not the cringeworthy part. Having failed at his attempt to summon the army with the shofar, that first man will pass the horn to the next for his shot at group glory. The horn will then be passed to the next, then the next. Then, when everyone who wants a turn has had a turn, they will set the trumpet back down. There it will sit for a minute or two until the next group walks up, lifts the shofar, and begins passing it from one set of lips to the next. I'm getting a little squeamish just thinking about it. I imagine selling shofars will look very different in a post-COVID-19 world.

While the shofar is what is normally referred to by "trumpet" in the Bible, there is another kind of horn mentioned that is made of a very different material. In Numbers 10, the people of Israel are camped in the Wilderness of Sinai. God had given the law to Moses, and the people were getting anxious to move on. But to move that many people, the Lord knew that there would need to be some organization. So, to help with crowd control, He gave Moses a task.

> The Lord spoke to Moses, saying: "Make two silver trumpets for yourself; you shall make them of hammered work; you shall use them for calling the congregation and for directing the movement of the camps. When they blow

both of them, all the congregation shall gather before you at the door of the tabernacle of meeting. But if they blow only one, then the leaders, the heads of the divisions of Israel, shall gather to you. When you sound the advance, the camps that lie on the east side shall then begin their journey. When you sound the advance the second time, then the camps that lie on the south side shall begin their journey; they shall sound the call for them to begin their journeys. And when the assembly is to be gathered together, you shall blow, but not sound the advance. The sons of Aaron, the priests, shall blow the trumpets; and these shall be to you as an ordinance forever throughout your generations.

"When you go to war in your land against the enemy who oppresses you, then you shall sound an alarm with the trumpets, and you will be remembered before the LORD your God, and you will be saved from your enemies. Also in the day of your gladness, in your appointed feasts, and at the beginning of your months, you shall blow the trumpets over your burnt offerings and over the sacrifices of your peace offerings; and they shall be a memorial for you before your God: I am the LORD your God" (Numbers 10:1-10).

Two trumpets were to be crafted from pure silver. Rather than looking like what you might find today in a school marching band, these would more closely resemble heraldry trumpets. They were likely long and straight with a gradual flare at the end. Picture in your mind a medieval king returning home to his kingdom. The trumpeters would stand on top of the castle walls and blast out the sound of their sovereign's arrival on their long, brightly polished horns. These are the type of trumpets that God commanded Moses to make. Not ones to play a song, but ones to serve a more practical purpose.

The immediate reasons for creating these instruments are spelled out in Numbers 10:2—they were "for calling the congregation and for directing the movement of the camps." Depending on whether it was one trumpet sounding or two, or the trumpeters were playing in unison or in a harmony, or they gave one long blast or a certain series of notes, the people could discern whether God was calling a meeting or telling them that it was time to start moving down the road. There was also a specific cadence that served as an alarm, letting the Israelites know that an enemy was approaching. These were real trumpets serving a real-world purpose for God's people. However, that doesn't preclude them from also being something more.

A SHADOW OF SOMETHING GREATER

Occasionally in the Bible, God will introduce a person or event or item that we will later discover has more significance than we originally anticipated. These are sometimes called types or representations or shadows. In my previous book, *The Day Approaching*, I presented the Old Testament feasts as shadow celebrations representing greater future events. Passover found its fulfillment in the crucifixion of Christ. The Feast of Unleavened Bread was satisfied in the perfect, sinless life of the Bread of Life, Jesus Christ. The Feast of Firstfruits was a shadow of the resurrection of our Lord, whom Paul describes as "the firstfruits of those who have fallen asleep" (1 Corinthians 15:20), indicating that we, too, will one day rise up in like manner from the grave. The Feast of Weeks, remembered over Pentecost, was expressed when the Holy Spirit was poured out upon the church. The Feast of Trumpets is finding current fulfillment in the signs all around us announcing the soon coming of our Lord. The Day of Atonement and the Feast of Tabernacles or Booths are still awaiting their realities, when, respectively, all Israel comes to Christ and when the church and all who follow the Lord will dwell together with Him in the millennial kingdom. For each of these events, something lesser is established that will find its greater counterpart in the future.

There are instances in Scripture when people are types or representations of something to come. The prophet Malachi recorded the words of the LORD of hosts:

> Behold, I will send you Elijah the prophet
> Before the coming of the great and dreadful
>   day of the LORD.

And he will turn
The hearts of the fathers to the children,
And the hearts of the children to their fathers,
Lest I come and strike the earth with a curse
    (Malachi 4:5-6).

Before the Messiah is revealed and the day of the Lord comes, Elijah will return. Because of this promise from God, a representative chair is set out for the prophet at every Seder meal. Jews will tell you that it is impossible for Jesus to be the promised Messiah because that chair is still empty—Elijah is still missing. No Elijah, no Messiah.

But Elijah *has* returned—and the Jewish people missed him. When the disciples were questioning Jesus about this very subject, Jesus responded,

> "Indeed, Elijah is coming first and will restore all things. But I say to you that Elijah has come already, and they did not know him but did to him whatever they wished. Likewise the Son of Man is also about to suffer at their hands." Then the disciples understood that He spoke to them of John the Baptist (Matthew 17:11-13).

Jesus tells the disciples that the Elijah the Jews should have been waiting for was not a literal Elijah, but a type—a representation. While the Old Testament Elijah proclaimed the coming of God for judgment, the New Testament Elijah—John the Baptist—proclaimed the coming of God for salvation.

There are also times when God will use things as shadows or types. This is the case for the two silver trumpets. Yes, they were actual trumpets that served a practical purpose. But they also represented something much greater. To discover this alternate identity, let's first look at their purpose.

A trumpet blast was primarily sounded to direct people's attention. If they heard the sound of a horn echoing through the city, they would stop what they were doing and listen. They knew that trumpets weren't sounded frivolously. If someone was blowing one or more horns, there had to be a reason.

Second, the trumpets sounded to call a gathering of the people. In Numbers 10:3, the Lord says, "When they blow both of them, all the congregation shall gather before you at the door of the tabernacle of meeting." When the horns sounded a specific cadence, the people left what they were doing and made their way to the tabernacle.

Third, these trumpets could be sounded to announce the arrival of a dignitary—again, like the heralds of old.

Finally, the trumpets can be blown to direct the people either in warfare or during a journey. One series of notes meant attack, another meant shift right, another meant retreat to safety.

A call to attention, to gather together, to announce someone's coming, or to direct the people—each one of these purposes can be linked to future events. The sounding of trumpets at the rapture, when Jesus returns to gather His church and take it to be with Him, and the second coming, that remarkable day when He steps foot again on the Mount of Olives with the church in tow in order to establish His kingdom on earth, contain elements of all four of the purposes for trumpets. But two of the above stated purposes are more evident in these events than the others.

Paul wrote to the church in Thessalonica about that wonderful moment when we will be taken up to meet Jesus in the clouds: "The Lord Himself will descend from heaven with a shout, with the voice of an archangel, and with the trumpet of God. And the dead in Christ will rise first. Then we who are alive and remain shall be caught up together with them in the clouds to meet the Lord in the air. And thus we shall always be with the Lord" (1 Thessalonians 4:16-17). At the rapture, Jesus will descend, the archangel will let out a holler, and a trumpet will echo through the heavens.

When Jesus returns a second time—this journey lasting all the way down to ground level—the trumpet will once more be heard, only this time it will sound throughout the earth. Jesus said:

> Immediately after the tribulation of those days the sun will
> be darkened, and the moon will not give its light; the stars
> will fall from heaven, and the powers of the heavens will
> be shaken. Then the sign of the Son of Man will appear

in heaven, and then all the tribes of the earth will mourn, and they will see the Son of Man coming on the clouds of heaven with power and great glory. And He will send His angels with a great sound of a trumpet, and they will gather together His elect from the four winds, from one end of heaven to the other (Matthew 24:29-31).

The heavenly trumpets will sound to announce the coming of our Lord at the rapture and at the second coming. They will also signal the coming together of His people—first, the church at the rapture will gather to Christ, then the saved Jews and any others who have come to Christ during the tribulation will congregate as Jesus returns to earth a second time with His bride, the church. Announcing and gathering—these are the two key purposes of the trumpets. But what about the attention-getting and directing functions? It is in these two roles that I see the specific typing of the two silver trumpets.

A CALL TO ATTENTION

We live in a very distracted and distracting world. Work, family, entertainment—there are so many voices that are calling for our attention. But this is nothing new. People have always found reasons to focus on the day-to-day of life and ignore the big picture. This is one of Satan's great tools against us. As long as we are looking at ourselves and our own busyness, our eyes are not on God.

Every now and then, news will come out of California of a highway accident involving dozens of vehicles. The cause is not snow or ice. These incidents take place on days when the Central Valley tule fog is at its worst. The tule, from which this fog derives its name, is a marsh reed that is prevalent in that region. When the conditions are just right, a thick, opaque, airborne moisture rises from these marshes and settles in—a joy for the fruit farmers, but a nightmare for motorists. Most drivers know to slow way down on foggy days, but there always seem to be those who feel they have X-ray vision that enables them to see through the white blanket. All it takes is one of these reckless road warriors to collide with the rear end of a car that suddenly appears in the cloud in front of them for a chain-reaction accident to start. The drivers behind them will not be expecting cars to be stopped on the road, so they'll plow into the bad driver's back end. Then the next car will hit, then the next, then the next. Sadly, there is no way to warn the oncoming cars and trucks about the danger that lies just ahead.

Warning is the job of the trumpets—to blow the signal, to get the attention of those who can't see or who are too distracted to notice the peril that is just up the road. It is to wake them up from their ignorance and apathy. God has created His trumpets to tell the world, "Stop! Wake up and turn around before it's too late!"

But what, you may be wondering, do these trumpets look like to us today? How can you recognize them or hear their sound? To understand this, there is something that you must first realize: These trumpets are not a *what*, but a *who*.

God's First Trumpet: Israel

There are two witnesses that God has called to get the attention of the world's population and point everyone to Himself. The first of these testifiers is Israel. "'You are My witnesses,' says the LORD, 'and My servant whom I have chosen, that you may know and believe Me, and understand that I am He. Before Me there was no God formed, nor shall there be after Me'" (Isaiah 43:10). The Lord looked over all time and all people, and He decided that this one nation would be singled out from all others. God didn't choose them because He was lonely and wanted companionship. Nor was His desire to create a spiritually elite nation that could lord their God-relationship over everyone else. Instead, His decision to make Israel His chosen people was as much about benefitting the rest of the world as it was about that one singled-out nation. When God made His covenant with Abraham, we see His blessing directed both within Israel and without:

Now the LORD had said to Abram:

"Get out of your country,
From your family

And from your father's house,
To a land that I will show you.
I will make you a great nation;
I will bless you
And make your name great;
And you shall be a blessing.
I will bless those who bless you,
And I will curse him who curses you;
And in you all the families of the earth shall be blessed"
(Genesis 12:1-3).

God's promise was that Abraham's descendants, Israel, would be blessed by Him, and that He would, in turn, bless the rest of the world through Israel. What did this blessing look like? First, it is from Israel that salvation would come to mankind. "Listen to Me, you stubbornhearted, who are far from righteousness: I bring My righteousness near, it shall not be far off; My salvation shall not linger. And I will place salvation in Zion, for Israel My glory" (Isaiah 46:12-13). When the Savior finally arrived on the scene, He came from Israel. Jesus was a Jew who dealt primarily with other Jews during His three-year ministry. And it was in Jerusalem that He was crucified, paying the price for our sins and opening the door for our salvation. If you are looking for the people and the place of salvation, both are found in the nation of Israel.

It is also through Israel that God first offered His written Word. From the detailed historical accounts to the beauty of the poetic books to the practical truths of the wisdom collections to the hope and warnings found within the prophets, humanity owes a debt of gratitude to the Jewish people for being the communicators of God's message to His creation.

Israel was given the responsibility to be a witness for God—to direct this world to the Father. Through how they lived and worshipped and obeyed and loved, they were to be the living representatives of the Creator on this earth. But instead of embodying this wonderful purpose, Israel infamously crashed and burned. The people sinned, rebelled, and ran away from their Lord who had blessed them so wonderfully.

*Israel and the church are the only two
groups of people whom God calls His witnesses.*

God's Second Trumpet: The Church

Enter God's second trumpet—the church. Just before Jesus ascended to heaven, He told the disciples, "You shall receive power when the Holy Spirit has come upon you; and you shall be witnesses to Me in Jerusalem, and in all Judea and Samaria, and to the end of the earth" (Acts 1:8). In the same way that Israel was meant to be God's witness to the world, He then passed this role on to the church. It is now from the church that the world hears about the truth of salvation through Jesus Christ, and it is from the church that the second collection of writings, the New Testament, was added to God's Word.

Israel and the church are the only two groups of people whom God calls His witnesses. While both were called to be the Lord's trumpets, the ways they sounded out have been different. Israel had much more of a passive testimony. The people demonstrated God simply by being. As they lived generation to generation, God was able to show who He was—His love, power, forgiveness, grace, mercy, and judgment. All His character and attributes were at some point demonstrated in His interactions with the nation. There were certainly some occasions when Israel was commanded to overtly preach God's message to the nations—such as God's call for Jonah to warn Nineveh that His judgment was coming. Jonah had other plans and hopped a ship headed the opposite direction. One storm and a big fish Uber later, Jonah was walking through the Assyrian capital smelling of stale seafood and warning the citizens to repent. But for the most part, Israel was called to be a living testimony of God.

One only need go back to the mandate that Jesus gave to the disciples prior to His ascension to see how different the church's calling was. This fledgling group of believers was to serve as witnesses to the ends of the earth. This charge is clearly stated in Matthew's account of this Great Commission, where Jesus told the disciples, "Go therefore and make disciples of all the nations, baptizing them in the name of the Father and of the Son and of the Holy Spirit, teaching them to observe all things that I have commanded you; and lo, I am with you always, even to the end of the age" (Matthew 28:19-20). While Israel was called to *be*, the church was told to *go*.

Not only are the methodologies of the witnesses different, so are the primary messages of Israel and the church. Israel announced the existence of God. The nation provided opportunities for God to demonstrate His character. It is through Israel that we see God is faithful, all-knowing, all-powerful, and everywhere present. The message of the church is more, "Okay, now that you know who this God is, here's your heads-up that He's on His way." These messages are not mutually exclusive. There is plenty of "God is coming, so you better get right with Him now" in the Old Testament, and there is no shortage of "Here's who our wonderful Lord is" found in the New. But before you warn people that someone is coming, you need to let them know who that someone is.

A DEEPER LOOK

When God told Moses to build two silver trumpets, He was creating a type—a shadow—of a bigger reality. Israel and the church were going to be His witnesses to wake up the people of the world to the reality of who God is and to warn them of His coming. Now that we know the purpose of the trumpets, let's take a deeper look at the details of these instruments.

First, notice that there are only two. God could have made three or five or seven or twenty. Instead, He just called for two. In the Bible, this is a number of union. There are two testaments that make up one Bible. The commandments, written on two tablets, comprise one law. During creation, after declaring everything to be good, God came to Adam. In a world of twos—two cows, two zebras, two elephants—there was only one "one." God said, "It is not good that man should be alone; I will make him a helper comparable to him" (Genesis 2:18). So, a quick nap and one rib removal later, the one had been made two. And here is where God's brilliance comes into full display. Now that the one was two, God instituted a plan for the two to again become one: "Therefore a man shall leave his father and mother and be joined to his wife, and they shall become one flesh" (Genesis 2:24).

This union is also found with the two trumpets. The two sound the testimony of the same God. Both find their origin in Abraham—Israel finds its physical origin in him, and the church its spiritual origin. And like Adam and Eve, these two will one day be made one. However, unlike what many believe, this union has not yet occurred. The union of Israel and the church will not come until there is a new heaven and a new earth—when there is no more need for a sun and moon and stars for light because God will be our light (Jeremiah 31:35-36; Revelation 21:23). We will deal with the current distinction between Israel and the church much more in the chapters ahead.

A second fact to consider about these trumpets is the material they are made from. Why are they made of silver? If they are so important and precious to God, why would He not make them out of gold? It's because silver better defines who we are. Silver is precious, but it is not the perfection of gold. Israel and the church are both very precious to God, but they are not perfect. And just like silver cannot make itself gold, Israel and the church cannot make themselves perfect. That is something that only God can do.

This is a truth that is a stumbling block to many Jews. A law-based belief system says, "You work hard enough, you'll reach perfection." But that's a losing proposition. You don't have to go to the New Testament to see that perfection will always be beyond reach. Even under the law, King Solomon wrote, "There is not a just man on earth who does good and does not sin" (Ecclesiastes 7:20). Still, the cross is an affront to the Jewish mindset because it says that forgiveness can only be received and not earned. No matter how hard you polish the silver, you will never find gold underneath.

This is true, also, for many who walk through the doorways of churches every week. They are trying to prove themselves to God through serving or giving or by making sure their good deeds outweigh their bad deeds. Again, this will never work, as Peter made clear when he said, "There is no other name under heaven given among men by which we must be saved" (Acts 4:12). There is no other name—that includes our own.

Our meaning and purpose and reason
for existence is only found outside of
ourselves—in the person of Jesus Christ.

The final part of the trumpet that bears discussion is the mouthpiece. A trumpet will not sound by itself. No matter how fine the craftsmanship, no matter how precious the metal, unless air is passed through the mouthpiece of a trumpet, it is no better than a heavy, expensive doorstop. The lips that press against these two silver trumpets are God's. It is His breath that passes through and sounds the beautiful notes. Israel and the church can do nothing on their own. They are just the vessels. It is only when the breath of God passes through them that they will play as He wants them to play. How sad it is to hear Jews and Christians boast of their identities, as if in themselves they are something special. Our meaning and purpose and reason for existence is only found outside of ourselves—in the person of Jesus Christ.

God's breath doesn't just give the trumpets voice, it gives them life. How has Israel survived over the millennia? Through persecution and pogrom, expulsion and genocide, nation after nation and leader after leader has sought to destroy that which God has created. The same was true for the church through most of its existence, and still is today in many parts of the world. Yet the Spirit of God—His breath passing through these trumpets—has sustained them.

Where can we find the breath of God? When we trust Christ for the forgiveness of our sins, we don't just receive salvation but also the Holy

Spirit. He is the gift given to all who believe. "Do you not know that you are the temple of God and that the Spirit of God dwells in you?" (1 Corinthians 3:16). The Spirit is the breath of God that sustains our souls, even when our bodies fail.

There is another source where we can find that life-supporting, witness-giving breath. "All Scripture is breathed out by God and profitable for teaching, for reproof, for correction, and for training in righteousness, that the man of God may be complete, equipped for every good work" (2 Timothy 3:16-17 ESV). It is in the Bible that we find God's exhalation. His words were sounded through His instruments and written down for us to hear any time that we desire.

Sadly, the reason so many churches are sounding foul notes is because they have strayed from the Bible to a feel-good, emotion-based theology. How can someone searching for the one true God find Him in a church where the Bible is mentioned only once or twice in a sermon, and even then only to back up a point that the pastor had already predetermined to make? The same is true of us as individuals. Unless we spend time each day filling ourselves with the Bible—the breath of God—we will never be able to sound the alarm to this world, nor will we be able to accurately represent who the Lord truly is.

WHAT SOUND ARE YOU MAKING?

If Israel and the church are the two trumpets, then only since 1948 have both trumpets sounded together. Until that point, there was only one playing at a time. In the Old Testament, Israel sounded God's fanfare. Since Pentecost, God has pressed His lips against the mouthpiece of the church. But when Israel again became a nation in 1948, suddenly the two trumpets united in a sonorous, if still imperfect, sound. Israel is once again demonstrating the power and character of the Lord by its very existence and by the amazing revitalization of the land. A key phrase repeated throughout the book of Ezekiel is "then they will know that I am the LORD." When you read Ezekiel 36–37, then look at the nation of Israel today, it is very evident that the Lord of all is alive and well and working in the world. Meanwhile, the church is continuing in its mandate to spread the gospel throughout the world. Two trumpets—separate, but still sounding together their unique divine tunes.

This is where our challenge comes in. Paul asked the question, "If the trumpet makes an uncertain sound, who will prepare for battle?" (1 Corinthians 14:8). What kind of sound are you making? When your neighbor or coworker or family member speaks with you, are they hearing the song of the Lord or just more worldly noise? We are to be the watchmen from Ezekiel 3:16-21. We are called to alert the lost about who God is and what is about to happen. The only way we can make sure that our sound is loud and our notes are true is to be daily in the Word of God and in prayer. This will allow the Spirit of God to fill our minds and His breath to fill our lungs. That is when all those around us will hear the trumpets of God in all we say and do.

CHAPTER 3

GETTING THE FULL PICTURE

God's Plan of Both/And Rather than Either/Or

A young boy sits three steps up on a cement stairway leading to an apartment building. Leaning against the gray balusters of the handrail, he digs his fingers into a peanut butter jar and transfers the contents into his mouth. Above him, an Italian man in a tweed suit walks through the front doors intent on unwrapping a bar of chocolate. His foot connects with a roller skate that has been carelessly abandoned in an unfortunate location. Down he tumbles toward the boy—legs and arms flailing and candy flying.

Landing in a heap on the sidewalk below, the man immediately begins searching for his precious chocolate. Forget checking himself for injuries or seeing if the boy was harmed in any way—he had to have his candy. Then he spots it, broken and firmly planted into the jar of peanut butter. Snatching it up, he accuses the boy, "You've got peanut butter on my chocolate." To which the surprised boy responds, "You've got chocolate in my peanut butter."

The boy then pulls a wedge of chocolate from his jar and the two aggrieved parties each take a bite. Their faces light up in amazement.

"Bravissimo," exclaims the Italian. "Yeah," agrees the child. An announcer's voice celebrates the union of the two flavors, "Two great tastes that taste great together—Reese's Peanut Butter Cups." The television commercial ends at a point later in the day with the man opening a bright orange package of Reese's and offering the boy a peanut butter cup as the two walk happily down the street together.

Of course, this advertisement leaves us with many questions. Did the Italian man and the boy know each other prior to this encounter? Where were the two strolling off to at the end of the ad? And what kind of parent sends their kid outside with a full jar of peanut butter and no spoon? Or what kind of parent sends their kid outside with a full jar of peanut butter, period?

Because these questions have continued unanswered since this commercial first aired in 1972, it's likely our curiosity will remain unsatisfied. But the message of the advertisement is clear. Both the man and the boy were content with their separate treats. The boy was all about his peanut butter, while the man was fully absorbed in his chocolate. Peanut butter is for peanut butter lovers and chocolate is for chocolate addicts, and never the twain shall meet. In their minds, chocolate and peanut butter were an either/or arrangement. However, by accident, these two snack connoisseurs discovered that while either/or can be fine, both/and can be better.

For many, when they look at Israel and the church, they do so through an either/or lens. Israel was God's chosen people. From Mount Sinai, God charged Moses with telling the Israelites, "If you will indeed obey My voice and keep My covenant, then you shall be a special treasure to Me above all people; for all the earth is Mine. And you shall be to Me a kingdom of priests and a holy nation" (Exodus 19:5-6). Sadly, Israel didn't act like God's special treasure. Instead, these people chased after every idol or god that winked its eye at them. Add to that their rejection of the promised Messiah—"He came to His own, and His own did not receive Him" (John 1:11)—and the conclusion that some people come to is that, because of their sin, God has rejected Israel.

Then they read the New Testament and see the new apple of God's eye—the church. "You are a chosen generation, a royal priesthood, a holy nation, His own special people, that you may proclaim the praises of Him who called you out of darkness into His marvelous light; who once were not a people but are now the people of God, who had not obtained mercy but now have obtained mercy" (1 Peter 2:9-10). Israel has been kicked to the curb, they say, and God has a new future bride that's caught His attention. Exodus 19 said that Israel was once a "kingdom of priests," but now the church is a "royal priesthood." Israel once was a "holy nation," but now the church is the new "holy nation." Israel once was God's "special treasure," but now the church is made up of His "own special people."

Israel was once God's chosen people, but now the church is the "chosen generation." This is either/or thinking, and it is neither necessary nor is it biblical. Both/and is so much better. In fact, for the prophecies of both the Old and the New Testament to be literally borne out, a both/and interpretation of Scripture is absolutely essential.

God selected Israel with the intent that it would become His vessel for approaching the rest of the world with His truth and salvation.

A GOD OF SECOND CHANCES

One of the great misunderstandings of the Jewish people and the church is that God chose Israel because of who Israel was. It's as if God looked ahead at the descendants of Abraham and was stunned and amazed. He decided that these future generations would be such wonderful examples of holiness and righteousness that they deserved His blessings to be poured out on them. However, as we saw earlier, the choosing of the Jewish people was less for that single nation than it was for the rest of the nations. God selected Israel with the intent that it would become His vessel for approaching the rest of the world with His truth and salvation.

This same purpose also applies to the church. Being a Christian has less to do with our own eternity than it does the eternities of others. We are certainly blessed with the promise of heaven in our future and God's presence in the here and now. But if that's where our perspective of Christianity ends, then we are missing God's greater plan and His calling for us. We are saved for a purpose. We are saved for service. Israel was God's way to reflect Himself to the world. The church is His chosen vessel to tell the world the good news that Jesus Christ has paid the price for their sins.

If God's timeline has moved on from Israel's reflection of God to the church's intentional witness, then this begs the question: Is Israel now irrelevant? Has the nation accomplished its task, now passing the baton to the church? Sometimes intentionally and other times unintentionally, Israel did an excellent job showing the world God's character. What does God's omnipotence look like? Look at the Hebrews escaping Egypt. Through Moses, the Lord told Pharaoh in the midst of the series of plagues, "For this purpose I have raised you up, that I may show My power in you, and that My name may be declared in all the earth" (Exodus 9:16). In the judgment against Egypt and in God's subsequent protection of Israel in the wilderness, His power over rulers and nations and nature was clearly demonstrated.

Are you wondering what God's patience looks like—not just with nations, but on an individual level? After the horrific reign of King Manasseh over Judah—a period filled with idol worship and bloodshed and child sacrifice—God was ready to bring a much-deserved judgment on His wayward people.

> The LORD spoke by His servants the prophets, saying, "Because Manasseh king of Judah has done these abominations (he has acted more wickedly than all the Amorites who were before him, and has also made Judah sin with his idols), therefore thus says the LORD God of Israel: 'Behold, I am bringing such calamity upon Jerusalem and Judah, that whoever hears of it, both his ears will tingle'" (2 Kings 21:10-12).

Ear-tingling judgment—not an experience I want to be around for. As the Lord prepared this coming destruction, Manasseh died, followed quickly by his son and successor, Amon, who was assassinated by his servants after only two years on the throne.

Next to ascend the throne was eight-year-old Josiah, a young boy who was determined to be different than his father and grandfather. Instead, he had his eyes set on the godly reign of his great-grandfather, King Hezekiah. He sought God the best he could while still under regency, too young to make his own decisions so most of his decisions were made for him. When he finally came into his own, he began a restoration process of the Temple during which the Book of the Law was rediscovered. Hearing of this wonderful find, Josiah immediately asked that it be read to him, and he was devastated by what he heard. As the priest read, the king realized just how far the nation had fallen from God's standard. Josiah was broken, and he repented in sackcloth and ashes for himself and for his people.

When the Lord saw the young king's attitude of humility, He sent word saying,

> Thus says the LORD God of Israel: "Concerning the words which you have heard—because your heart was tender, and you humbled yourself before the LORD when you heard what I spoke against this place and against its inhabitants, that they would become a desolation and a curse, and you tore your clothes and wept before Me, I also have heard you," says the LORD. "Surely, therefore, I will gather you to your fathers, and you shall be gathered to your grave in peace; and your eyes shall not see all the calamity which I will bring on this place" (2 Kings 22:18-20).

God's character demands justice for sin, and the kingdom of Judah was due for a serious helping of divine justice. However, the long-suffering patience the Lord showed to King Josiah demonstrated that the repentance and humility of one man can stay the powerful hand of God. Divine mercy and grace substituted joy for sorrow, peace for punishment. God's love for one young man whose heart was directed toward

Him resulted in life and hope for all the people in Judah—at least for the duration of the youthful monarch's lifetime.

God's treatment of the Israelites showed the nations who He was. Those times when they were deeply committed to the Lord allowed Him to demonstrate all those attributes that warm our hearts. The loving, compassionate nature of the Lord can be seen in the rescue of Israel from Egypt, in the conquering of the Promised Land under Joshua, in the godly reigns of David and Jehoshaphat and Hezekiah and Josiah, in the wisdom and safe-keeping of Daniel, in the elevation and courage of Queen Esther, in the postexilic return of the Jews to Jerusalem under Zerubbabel and Nehemiah, and in so many other accounts.

God's love and faithfulness to His promises will not
allow Him to cast aside His chosen people for good.

Sadly, those best of times were often overshadowed by Israel's all-too-regular worst of times. From the golden calf rebellion in the wilderness to the ever-worsening spiral into sin during the time of the judges to the complete lack of any godly monarch in the northern kingdom of Israel, the characteristics of God most often seen in the Bible's history books and prophetic writings are His indignation, His sorrow, and His judgment. After the fall of Jerusalem, the word of the Lord came to Ezekiel, saying,

> I will make the land most desolate, her arrogant strength shall cease, and the mountains of Israel shall be so desolate that no one will pass through. Then they shall know that I am the LORD, when I have made the land most desolate because of all their abominations which they have committed (Ezekiel 33:28-29).

Judgment came upon Jerusalem, demonstrating to the surviving Jews and the rest of the nations that there is a holy, all-powerful God in heaven.

But if we leave Israel in judgment, as so many do who reject God's people today, then we are missing the best part of the story. We are also not getting the full reflection of who God truly is. The Father does not abandon His children. His love and faithfulness to His promises will not allow Him to cast aside His chosen people for good. Just three chapters after the pronouncement of His judgment in Ezekiel 33, we read these words that God spoke to the prophet:

> I will take you from among the nations, gather you out of all countries, and bring you into your own land. Then I will sprinkle clean water on you, and you shall be clean; I will cleanse you from all your filthiness and from all your idols. I will give you a new heart and put a new spirit within you; I will take the heart of stone out of your flesh and give you a heart of flesh. I will put My Spirit within you and cause you to walk in My statutes, and you will keep My judgments and do them. Then you shall dwell in the land that I gave to your fathers; you shall be My people, and I will be your God…Then the nations which are left all around you shall know that I, the LORD, have rebuilt the ruined places and planted what was desolate. I, the LORD, have spoken it, and I will do it (Ezekiel 36:24-28,36).

Our God is a God of second, third, and fourth chances. In fact, as long as we repent and turn back to Him, He will always be found by us. How do we know this? We look at the reflection of His character through His chosen nation—Israel.

THE STEADFAST LOVE OF THE FATHER

At the advent of the New Testament era, Israel as a nation was still in rebellion against God. However, it was a more subtle rebellion than the eras of the judges or the kings. On the outside, all appeared to be perfect. There was worship in the Temple. There was a passion for the law. People were gathering for the feasts and bringing their sacrifices, and they were carrying out their duties. But in the midst of carrying out the law of God, the nation had forgotten God Himself. They followed a religion—a system of rules and regulations. In short, nothing had changed over previous centuries—they had once again put another god, the law, ahead of the true God.

Jesus saw that the Jewish religious leaders were still stuck in the mindset of their ancestors. When the scribes and Pharisees called Jesus out for letting His disciples eat without going through the traditional ritual of washing, Jesus called them hypocrites. Then He quoted the Father speaking through the prophet Isaiah, saying, "These people draw near to Me with their mouth, and honor Me with their lips, but their heart is far from Me. And in vain they worship Me, teaching as doctrines the commandments of men" (Matthew 15:8-9). The Lord had made the law to help guide the conduct of His people, but His people had turned around and made the law their god.

The people that God had chosen to reflect Himself were caught up in sinful idolatry. What hope was there for the Jews and for the rest of the world who had been depending upon them for their glimpse of the true God? In stepped the church. God wanted to communicate His grace, His mercy, His solution for sin, and His plan to bring salvation to the world. Suddenly, Israel, rather than being the giver of the message, became the receiver of the message.

Again, there are those who say that because the people of Israel failed in their mission, God is done with them. That's not a new perspective. It's been around almost as long as the church has been in existence. After Pentecost, when the church was first born, it was purely Jewish. As a result, there was an initial heavily anti-Gentile bias. But through the experiences and testimonies of Peter and Paul, the church came to see that Christ died for all. Thus, Paul wrote, "We conclude that a man is justified by faith apart from the deeds of the law. Or is He the God of the Jews only? Is He not also the God of the Gentiles? Yes, of the Gentiles also, since there is one God who will justify the circumcised by faith and the uncircumcised through faith" (Romans 3:28-30).

For some Gentiles, however, the pendulum swung to the point that the Jews began to experience the denigration. Word of this anti-Semitic attitude spreading through the Roman church led Paul to address it head on. "I say then, has God cast away His people? Certainly not! For I also am an Israelite, of the seed of Abraham, of the tribe of Benjamin. God has not cast away His people whom He foreknew" (Romans 11:1-2). I am sometimes amazed at how various pastors and theologians can look at this passage and say, "Well, sure, Paul clearly states that God has not cast away His people. But that doesn't really mean what it looks like it means."

Really? How much clearer can Paul be? If he were a teenager today, he would probably clap with each syllable: "Has God cast away His people? Cer-[clap]-tain-[clap]-ly-[clap] not-[clap]!"

Paul then went a step further, telling them that not only should they not be dogging on the Jews; they should be thanking them. He said to the Christians in Rome, "I say then, have they stumbled that they should fall? Certainly not! But through their fall, to provoke them to jealousy, salvation has come to the Gentiles. Now if their fall is riches for the world, and their failure riches for the Gentiles, how much more their fullness!" (Romans 11:11-12).

The church the "Gentile" voice of God, as opposed to Israel's "Jewish" voice of God has now been given both the message of the gospel and the mission of the gospel. This mission is twofold. It is to communicate the gospel in "Jerusalem, and in all Judea and Samaria, and to the end of the earth" (Acts 1:8). And it is to provoke the Jews to jealousy through the church picking up the job that Israel had essentially been fired from. But just because Israel was fired doesn't mean it was discarded.

Consider a man who owns a business. It is a communications company created to spread a very specific message. This man has two sons. He decides to put his older son in charge of the company. This young man tries leading the business, but he is too preoccupied with other things to do a good job. While he has some successes, he has many more failures. Eventually, the elder son's leadership becomes so negligent that the father is forced to sack him from his position. In his place, he puts the younger son. Under the new leadership, the company turns around and the message the father created the business to communicate begins to spread rapidly. Eventually the company goes global and has thousands of employees.

This scenario brings up some questions. First, when the older son was fired from his job, did he cease being a son? Did his father love him any less? Of course not. In fact, it probably broke the father's heart to have to do what he did. Second, how would the older son feel when he saw his younger brother stepping into his former position? Angry, jealous, sad—he may have even longed for another chance to do the job right.

This is what we see in Romans 11. And the great joy of this chapter is the promise that the older son will have that chance to serve again, this time alongside his brother. Once the church has completed the job it was called to do, Israel will be brought back into the "company." "I do not desire, brethren, that you should be ignorant of this mystery, lest you should be wise in your own opinion, that blindness in part has happened to Israel until the fullness of the Gentiles has come in. And so all Israel will be saved" (Romans 11:25-26). Either/or thinking says that there can only be one son at a time. Both/and allows that while there may only be one son in charge of the company, both sons can be recipients of the vast love of the Father.

GOD'S PERFECT TIMING

There was a time for the Jews, there currently is a time for the Gentiles, and at the second coming, there will be a time for both the Jews and Gentiles together. God's plans are based on order and on process. King Solomon wrote, "To everything there is a season, a time for every purpose under heaven" (Ecclesiastes 3:1). When God laid out His perfect plan for salvation, He did it in the right season—based on set times and boundaries.

Jesus came at the perfect time to fulfill the prophecies
that had been made about Him centuries before.

Regarding Jesus' birth, Paul wrote to the Galatians, "When the fullness of the time had come, God sent forth His Son, born of a woman, born under the law, to redeem those who were under the law, that we might receive the adoption as sons" (Galatians 4:4-5). Jesus came at the perfect time to fulfill the prophecies that had been made about Him centuries before. But why had God chosen that specific time to send His Son?

To know the definitive answer, we would have to get into the mind of God. However, based on history, we can do some speculating. From a logical perspective based on the Lord's desire to introduce His church to the world and spread the gospel rapidly, there was no better time in history for the arrival of the Messiah than the first and second centuries. This was the time of the *Pax Romana* (Latin for "Roman Peace"). Lasting from around 20 BC to AD 180, this was when the Roman Empire was at its strongest and most secure.

Certainly there were rebellions around the fringes of the empire—including a couple in Judaea—but for the most part, this was truly a time of peace. Because of this, travel was easy and relatively safe, whether by sea or on the well-built and well-used Roman roads. The empire's philosophy of sanctioning cultural and religious integrity among their conquered peoples, as long as it didn't interfere with Roman rule, created a relatively secure "Petri dish" for Christianity to grow in.

At no other time in ancient history could Paul have traveled as he did. At no other time would he have had such a vast array of people open to proselytization and a government willing to allow it. This is the background behind Paul's admonition to Timothy and the church at Ephesus:

> I exhort first of all that supplications, prayers, intercessions, and giving of thanks be made for all men, for kings and all who are in authority, that we may lead a quiet and peaceable life in all godliness and reverence. For this is good and acceptable in the sight of God our Savior, who desires all men to be saved and to come to the knowledge of the truth (1 Timothy 2:1-4).

Pray for kings and authorities to be able to keep the peace so we can quietly continue in our mission to spread the gospel throughout the Roman Empire. God sent His Son at just the right time!

God sets times. He set the time for the ministry of the Jews. He set the time for the ministry of the church. He has set the time for salvation and He has set the time for judgment. When Paul was in Athens speaking to the learned Greeks in the Areopagus, he said,

> He has made from one blood every nation of men to dwell on all the face of the earth, and has determined their pre-appointed times and the boundaries of their dwellings, so that they should seek the Lord, in the hope that they might grope for Him and find Him, though He is not far from each one of us (Acts 17:26-27).

God has set times and borders in order for people to find Him.

By the way, let me give you a little Bible-interpretation tip. Anytime you see the words "so that" (sometimes shortened to just "that"), you know either a purpose clause or a result clause is coming. God says, "I want you to do this, *so that* this might happen." "I have done this, *so that* this will be true." In the Gospel of John, you find a triple-dose of purpose clauses in the verses, "God so loved the world *that* He gave His only begotten Son, *that* whoever believes in Him should not perish but have everlasting life. For God did not send His Son into the world to condemn the world, but *that* the world through Him might be saved" (John 3:16-17). The three clauses tell us that as a result of God's love, He gave His Son. As a result of Him giving His Son, whoever believes will have eternal life. And the purpose of sending His Son was not to condemn but to save. So, when you're reading God's Word, keep your eyes open for "so that" and "that"—they typically explain the *whys* for God's *whats*.

Back to God's times—in the book of Romans we see that God has appointed a time for the church. But there is a period coming that He has already determined when He will turn His eyes back to Israel. When "the fullness of the Gentiles has come in" (Romans 11:25), that's when He will stir a mass revival amongst the remaining Jews. God is not done with them. Their time will come again.

SATAN'S LOSING STRATEGY

If I can recognize the coming revival among the Jews and you can recognize it, then do you know who else recognizes it? Satan. Remember, this is all part of God's grand plan of history. He is the God of the whole world, and He has laid out times from the beginning to the end. At the conclusion of the church age will come the rapture, the removal of the bride of Christ from the earth. This will soon be followed by the tribulation—seven years of God's discipline against Israel and His wrath against the world. It is at the end of this time that Christ will return to earth at the second coming, and all Israel will be saved.

After a bloody defeat in battle, Satan will be bound for 1,000 years during the millennial reign of Christ, at the end of which the devil will be released for a short time. He will stir up the masses against the Lord and will once again be soundly defeated, after which he will be cast into the lake of fire for eternity. We'll discuss these events in more detail later in this book. This is the plan that God has laid out step by step, leading to the end of Satan and the advent of the new heavens and the new earth. But what happens if a step is rendered impossible? If God is a God of order and He has prophesied His specific plan, then won't the removal of one step shut down the whole process because He can not go against His word?

Satan doesn't have the power to keep Christ from returning. The prophesied future military defeats demonstrate that the devil is not strong enough to stop the Lord in battle, let alone hold back His movements. In the timeline laid out above, what is the one vulnerable step? The salvation of Israel. What happens if there is no Israel left to be saved? The plan is short-circuited. God cannot remain true to His promise of a Jewish revival if there are no Jews, thereby halting His grand plan before the millennium. This means there can be no 1,000-year imprisonment, no final battle, and no lake of fire. It's a long shot, but it may be the only shot the devil thinks he has.

Time after time in history, Satan has worked through individuals and nations to attempt to destroy the chosen people of God:

Do not keep silent, O God!
Do not hold Your peace,
And do not be still, O God!
For behold, Your enemies make a tumult;
And those who hate You have lifted up their head.
They have taken crafty counsel against Your people,
And consulted together against Your sheltered ones.
They have said, "Come, and let us cut them off
    from being a nation,
That the name of Israel may be remembered no more"
    (Psalm 83:1-4).

The way Satan is fighting God is by fighting His "sheltered ones." From millennia of pogroms and persecutions to European expulsions and ghettos—from Nazi Germany to war after war against the Israelis from their Arabic neighbors, the devil has tried time after time after time to wipe out God's chosen people. But it is a losing proposition. First, because of God's never-ending love for Israel. "For thus says the LORD of hosts: 'He sent Me after glory, to the nations which plunder you; for he who touches you touches the apple of His eye'" (Zechariah 2:8).

Despite my time in the military, I am not a violent man. But my children are the apples of their father's eye. If someone were to harm them, the perpetrator would not want to see the man I would become. There are times when God has allowed nations to bring harm to Israel, but only for a time and only for a reason. Through it all, He has always been there to say, "Enough is enough."

---

*Israel is a reflection of God's love to the
whole world. Even when we rebel against
Him, He will never abandon us.*

The second reason that Satan fighting Israel is a losing proposition is that God uses the protection of His people to demonstrate who He is. Once again, we are back to God reflecting His character through the Jews. When God shelters His people, it's a bad rep for Satan. Rather than harming God, it displays His faithfulness and mercy and love. It shows everything that Satan is not. If Satan were able to come and take Israel away from God, then it would show that God is not taking care of His own. He is either powerless or too uncaring to keep them safe. But that is against His character. That is why Paul wrote, "If we are faithless, He remains faithful; He cannot deny Himself" (2 Timothy 2:13). We cannot measure God by the way we are. We measure Him by the way He is. His heart is not like our heart. Israel is a reflection of God's love to the whole world. Even when we rebel against Him, He will never abandon us.

GOD IS FAITHFUL
EVEN WHEN WE AREN'T

Look, I'm the last person to say that I know God perfectly and that I follow Him faithfully. I don't. But does that make the faithfulness of God of no use? The Bible says, "What if some did not believe? Will their unbelief make the faithfulness of God without effect? Certainly not! Indeed, let God be true but every man a liar" (Romans 3:3-4). Paul, who is a Jew, understands the irrevocable calling of God. Just before those verses, Paul had penned, "What advantage then has the Jew, or what is the profit of circumcision? Much in every way! Chiefly because to them were committed the oracles of God" (Romans 3:1-2). This was written during the church age, when some say that God had already rejected Israel. According to Replacement Theology, the time of the Jews had passed. If that were true, then in answer to the question, "What advantage then has the Jew…?," Paul likely would have answered, "Uh, none." Instead, what does he say? "Much!"

You can almost hear Paul's thoughts after verse two—*I know, I know, next you're going to tell me they don't believe.* Anticipating that response, he says in essence, "So what if they don't believe? Are you going to tell me that their disbelief is canceling the faithfulness of God? Is that really what you want to say?" The way God treats Israel demonstrates that He is the Truth. If He changed His mind about His chosen people, then it would make Him a liar. Men are liars; God is Truth.

Even when the Jews rejected Jesus, where in the Bible does He curse them? Even on the cross Jesus didn't curse them. And where in the Bible does Paul give up on the Jews and say, "Okay, that's it, guys. You've gone way too far this time"? Even up to the last chapter in Acts when he was delivered to Rome, where he would eventually be executed, he gathered the Jewish leaders together and said, "When the Jews spoke against [letting me go], I was compelled to appeal to Caesar, not that I had anything of which to accuse my nation. For this reason therefore I have called for you, to see you and speak with you, because for the hope of Israel I am bound with this chain" (Acts 28:19-20). It's not for the Gentiles or the church that he was in chains. It was for the hope of Israel.

God is faithful—He cannot deny Himself.
His love for His children is based solely
on His character, not on our actions.

The fact that God is still faithful to Israel despite the people's unbelieving state demonstrates the marvelous character of our Lord. Too many people focus on the unfaithfulness of Israel instead of on the faithfulness of God. In fact, it just might be that Israel is more effective at showing the glory of who our God is in their rebellion than they ever were when they were faithful.

Together—the church in its belief and Israel in its unbelief—these two chosen peoples are showing the full nature of who God is. Both are essential for seeing the complete picture. This is why Replacement Theology is so wrong. It plays right into Satan's hand by saying that God will abandon that which is His own. Those who hold to this view say that Israel was so bad that God cast the Jewish people aside and gave all their promises to the church. That's impossible. God is faithful—He cannot deny Himself. His love for His children is based solely on His character, not on our actions.

PART 2:

TWO DISTINCT PLANS

CHAPTER 4

A WIFE AND A BRIDE

The Unique Relationships of
Israel and the Church to God

I am a child of divorce. I was young when my parents decided they could no longer continue in their marriage. There was too much hurt, too much history for them to remain under the same roof. Their decision shook my world, along with that of my siblings. Ultimately, their split is what led me into the foster system and some of the most traumatic times of my life.

Divorce is a serious undertaking and its ramifications can be widespread and devastating. This is why it is so jarring to read God say, "Then I saw that for all the causes for which backsliding Israel had committed adultery, I had put her away and given her a certificate of divorce" (Jeremiah 3:8). God divorced His chosen people. No matter how bad they were, was there anything that they could have done that would demand that severe of a response? In a word, yes. Big time. In fact, the long-suffering patience of the Lord is the only reason it hadn't happened much sooner. Israel was unfaithful to her Husband in innumerable and extreme ways. So God said, "Because of your unfaithfulness, our marriage is at an end."

Sadly, there are many people who say that's when Israel's story finished. "See," they say, "God put aside Israel for good. In their place, He found a more faithful bride—the church." But they say this because either they have never read their whole Bible, or they don't understand the true character of God—or both. The Father sent Israel away, but for a reason and only for a season. And in His time, He will once again be united to His wife in a union that will last for eternity.

SET APART FOR GOD

From the beginning, God never intended for the people of Israel to be just like every other nation. They are special—chosen. Yet, as we mentioned in the previous chapter, their being singled out by God had nothing to do with them being good or great or worthy. The Jewish people's unique designation was not because of who they are, but because of who He is. All of you who lift Israel to superstar status—striving to emulate the Jewish people by following the feasts and laws, ensuring that you only call our Savior *Yeshua* and never that Gentile name *Jesus*—you need to step back and take a look at what you're doing. For some it almost becomes Israel worship. Don't worship Israel; worship the God of Israel.

God designed Israel to be different—to stand alone amongst the nations. "But, Amir, that sounds so sad. Isn't Israel lonely? Does Israel want some company, maybe to go out and grab a coffee and a falafel?" No, standing alone is the mandate of our people. Think about it: Being chosen to stand alone in a wicked world is actually a privilege. It is a high calling—a blessing from God. And there is a great benefit in being blessed by God, because how can anyone truly curse that which God blesses?

This is a point that the Lord brought home to King Balak of Moab using Balaam, a pagan prophet. King Balak had heard about how the God of Israel was leading His people though the wilderness and fighting their battles for them. The king understood that in the physical realm, there was no way that he could defeat Israel. He figured that if the physical path to attacking Israel was blocked, then he needed to change course. Just like when you are driving on a road and you hear on the radio that there is an accident ahead. If you're smart, you will pull off the highway and take a different course to your destination. When you're dealing with gods, fighting in the physical realm is a losing proposition. You've got to move into the realm of the spiritual. That is the road King Balak turned onto. If you can't beat the people of Israel with a sword or a machine gun or a tank or an F-16, then maybe you can defeat them with a curse.

By the way, the spiritual realm is no less dangerous than the physical. That's why we are told in Ephesians 6 to put on the armor of God— our helmet, our breastplate, holding our sword of God's Word in our hands. The Bible is a powerful weapon against our enemy. So when you go to the airport and they ask you if you are carrying a weapon in your bag—well, it's up to you what you say. In Israel, don't say, "Well, I do have my sword," because you'll quickly find yourself handcuffed to a table in a little white room with no windows.

King Balak sent far away for a well-known and powerful pagan prophet named Balaam. Sadly for Balaam, his fame has been greatly eclipsed through history by that of his talking donkey. Balak's messengers told Balaam that if he would pronounce a curse over the people of Israel, the king would pay him a large sum of money. Balaam wasn't so sure about this at first. He had heard of Jehovah God, and he didn't think it was too great of an idea to get into a scrape with Him. But, ultimately, God gave him the go-ahead, and Balaam set off on his overly verbal pack animal.

When Balaam and Balak finally met up, the king took the prophet up onto a mountain, where they could look down on the Israelites. Balak was rubbing his hands together, excited to hear the words of condemnation spew from Balaam's mouth. Instead, what he heard was,

> How shall I curse whom God has not cursed?
> And how shall I denounce whom the Lord
>   has not denounced?
> For from the top of the rocks I see him,
> And from the hills I behold him;
> There! A people dwelling alone,

Not reckoning itself among the nations
(Numbers 23:8-9).

Balaam was telling Balak, "I know that you are wanting a curse. Sorry, no can do. These people are not like all the other people. God has made them different. They are truly set apart." He completed his oracle, saying,

Who can count the dust of Jacob,
Or number one-fourth of Israel?
Let me die the death of the righteous,
And let my end be like his! (verse 10).

Balak was furious. He had paid handsomely for a curse, and instead, the Hebrews received a blessing. But Balaam couldn't do any differently. There is no way to curse the ones whom God has blessed. The Israelites are a different group of people—set apart—specially chosen by God.

"But, Amir, how can you say that the Jews are still special? Paul wrote to the Galatians that there is no more Jew or Gentile." True. The apostle wrote, "There is neither Jew nor Greek, there is neither slave nor free, there is neither male nor female; for you are all one in Christ Jesus" (Galatians 3:28; cf. Ephesians 2:14; Colossians 3:11). My question is, Why are you only reading the first twenty-three words of the verse, but skipping the last three? Those three are important too. "In Christ Jesus," Paul wrote, completing his thought.

When we become believers, we all become one in our Savior and part of the church. You may be an American believer or a Filipino believer or an Australian believer or a Ukrainian believer—yes, you may even be a Jewish believer. We are all together one in Christ. But apart from Christ, when we look at Israel in the context of the rest of the world, the Jews are separated and special. As I mentioned earlier, they are different for a reason and for a season.

THE GOD WHO KEEPS ISRAEL

Israel will not stand alone forever. But for now, there are marked differences that keep it estranged from the other nations. Again, we saw this earlier—Paul said, "What advantage then has the Jew, or what is the profit of circumcision? Much in every way! Chiefly because to them were committed the oracles of God. For what if some did not believe? Will their unbelief make the faithfulness of God without effect?" (Romans 3:1-3). Rome had an ethnically mixed church. In fact, there were likely many more Jews than Gentiles. That's why the letter to the Romans is filled with Old Testament references. Paul told the Roman church, "Yes, Israel is different. Yes, there is an advantage to being a Jew. Yes, God is handling the people in a unique way!"

God's plan has always been to let the nations see
who He is through how He handles Israel.

The fact that after 2,000 years of exile the Jewish people are now back in their land shows the hand of God. Not only are they home, but their culture and language have also returned. This is unheard of. No other nation on planet Earth has ever survived what Israel has. And it's not because Israel was strong and smart and beautiful and great. It's because God is strong. It's because God is smart. It's because God is beautiful and great. The God "who keeps Israel shall neither slumber nor sleep" (Psalm 121:4). He has had His active, mighty hand on His people from the beginning, and He has never completely removed it even through today. His plan has always been to let the nations see who He is through how He handles Israel.

You will not find another example of Paul writing quite as strongly as he did in Romans 9 when he spoke about the Jewish people. He began, "I tell the truth in Christ, I am not lying, my conscience also bearing me witness in the Holy Spirit, that I have great sorrow and continual grief in my heart" (verses 1-2). He started off telling everyone that what he was about to say was not from himself. This message was directly from the Holy Spirit. "So if you call me a liar, you need to realize that that you're actually calling the Holy Spirit a liar—not necessarily a good thing to do." Then Paul told the Romans that the truth he was about to reveal broke his heart.

I fully understand what Paul was saying here. Sorrow is what every believing Jew feels then they see unbelieving Jews still caught up in trying to establish their own righteousness. In fact, the heart of every believer should weep when they see the chosen people of God turning their back on the true Messiah. Instead of accepting Jesus Christ, they continue to wait with anticipation for a false messiah of their own making. The grief we feel should drive us to our knees and lead us to pray for the veil to be lifted from the hearts of the people of Israel so that they can see the hope that is found in Jesus.

But, even without the Messiah, Paul said that there is great advantage to being a Jew. It is to Israel "to whom pertain the adoption, the glory, the covenants, the giving of the law, the service of God, and the promises; of whom are the fathers and from whom, according to the flesh, Christ came, who is over all, the eternally blessed God. Amen" (Romans 9:4-5). Adoption, glory, covenants, law, service, and promises—all were gifts from God given to the Jews, and through the Jews to the rest of the nations. And there was one more very special gift. Like parents on Christmas morning who save the new bicycle for last, Paul built up his list to the coup d'grace. It was from the Jews that the world was given Jesus Christ. Look at how Paul described Him: "…who is over all, the eternally blessed God." If you have a problem with the deity of Jesus, then you have a problem with the Word of God. This truth could not be clearer.

ADDING TO, NOT REPLACING

God has used Israel to bless the world. But it wasn't just a pragmatic relationship. He didn't bring the Hebrews on His personal staff to carry out a job, then toss them aside when the task was done. Israel continues to be special in the eyes of God. When you became a believer, you did not replace Israel because God never had the intention of replacing the Jews. The Bible says the church has been "grafted in" to the tree. To be added is not to replace. The church is "in addition to," not "instead of."

> If the firstfruit is holy, the lump is also holy; and if the root is holy, so are the branches. And if some of the branches were broken off, and you, being a wild olive tree, were grafted in among them, and with them became a partaker of the root and fatness of the olive tree, do not boast against the branches. But if you do boast, remember that you do not support the root, but the root supports you (Romans 11:16-18).

Notice the phrases Paul used—"among them" and "with them"—not "in place of them." Israel was established as a separated, unique nation before God, and this continues to be so. The Jews are His chosen people. Is that me saying that, or is it the Word of God? Trust me, if there is one thing that the Israelis wish, it is that they were just like the other nations. My grandparents, who survived Auschwitz, once said to me, "We wish we were not the chosen people because we have been suffering for so long." We Jews would love to not be continually on the receiving end of attacks and persecution and hatred. The people of Israel have been saying, "Let's all live in harmony. Let us be part of the rest of the world. Let us join in this global effort to bring about peace."

There will be a day when this wish will be answered—when Israel will live in peace and harmony with the rest of the world. Unfortunately, this will not happen until the Jewish people cede their autonomy and allow the Antichrist to reign over them. He will lure them in with the promise of the Third Temple, and they'll jump at the chance. They'll think this great unifier is the best thing since lamb kebabs—at least until he walks into that shiny new Temple and declares himself to be god. That's when everything will collapse around the Jews and they will flee for the hills.

WHEN ALL ARE ONE IN CHRIST

For now, Israel will continue to maintain an existence separate from the rest of the world and the church. Is this separation from the church a permanent state? As we briefly noted in chapter 1, there is coming a day when Israel and the church will be united.

> Thus says the LORD,
> Who gives the sun for a light by day,
> The ordinances of the moon and the stars for
>   a light by night,
> Who disturbs the sea,
> And its waves roar
> (The LORD of hosts is His name):
> "If those ordinances depart
> From before Me, says the LORD,
> Then the seed of Israel shall also cease
> From being a nation before Me forever"
>   (Jeremiah 31:35-36).

Is God just giving us a hypothetical "if…then" statement? Is He simply being poetic, painting a verbal picture of a universe that will never be? Or could this passage be referring to an actual time when there will be no more moon, stars, or sun? Is there a coming era during which there will be no need for them because something else will be our source of light?

THE STREET GOES ONLY ONE WAY

At the end of time, God will make new heavens and a new earth. There will be a new Jerusalem, and all things will be made new. In this re-creation, there will be no need for rabbis or pastors or priests because everyone will already believe in Jesus Christ. And all will know God and understand His character and will have experienced His great plan of salvation. Thus, there will be no need for a separate nation or group to be a witness of Him and His character. This puts Israel and the church out of a job. It is at this time there will truly be no Jew nor Gentile because all will know Christ, and all will be one in Christ.

Until God makes new heavens and a new earth, however, the only shifting of categories between Israel and the church is when Jews move

into the church by believing in Jesus. I am one of those very few Jewish people who live in Israel who are not truly part of Israel, but instead,
belong to the church. Currently, there are around 20,000 of us. But
praise the Lord, He has brought me into His spiritual family. I have
been adopted. I am a new creation. It is no longer I who lives, but
Christ who lives in me.

There is no reciprocal movement of church to Jew, as much as some
denominations and Christians desire to make that switch. The street
goes only one way. Please, do not follow the teachings of those who
are trying to build up Jewish walls around the free gift of salvation.
They tell you that without following the Mosaic law, you are not good
enough. You need to keep the Sabbath. You need to follow the feasts.
These people are all part of the Jesus Plus movement. They say, "You
have to receive Jesus, plus you have to do this and this and this."

Israel and the church are two separated entities.
There will come a day when the two will be one.

Paul had to deal with these people everywhere he preached Jesus.
He would proclaim the gospel, plant a church, then move to the next
mission field. As soon as his feet reached outside a town's borders, the
Judaizers would swoop in and tell the church, "Oh yeah, Paul is great
and all. But he left a part out of his message—you need to be circumcised too."

Circumcision.

You know, it's one thing to tell an eight-day-old baby boy that he
needs to be circumcised. It's something very different to say that to a
thirty-eight-year-old man. All that newfound joy of the Lord quickly
goes away. The very first church council in history met to address these
Jesus Plus people who were teaching a false gospel. Salvation is by grace
through faith—period. This is true for the Jews and for the Gentiles.

Israel and the church are two separated entities. There will come a day when the two will be one. That day, however, is not today.

TWO KEY ILLUSTRATIONS

The Relationship Between God and Israel

In order to emphasize the depth of His love for both Israel and the church, God used two different very intimate relationships as illustrations. First, Scripture tells us that Jehovah made Israel His wife. The prophet Ezekiel presents a very tragic and graphic portrayal of God's relationship with Israel. Interestingly, this begins with a marriage:

> "When I passed by you again and looked upon you, indeed
> your time was the time of love; so I spread My wing over you
> and covered your nakedness. Yes, I swore an oath to you and
> entered into a covenant with you, and you became Mine,"
> says the Lord GOD (Ezekiel 16:8; cf. Deuteronomy 5:1-3).

Out of all the nations of the world, the Father chose the morally challenged Israel to be His wife. Using the words of a husband warning His wife against breaking her vows, God told the Jews, "You shall not go after other gods, the gods of the peoples who are all around you (for the LORD your God is a jealous God among you), lest the anger of the LORD your God be aroused against you and destroy you from the face of the earth" (Deuteronomy 6:14-15).

"Wait, Amir. God jealous? Isn't jealousy a bad thing?" It can be if it comes from a possessive and selfish heart. But God's jealousy is roused from a desire to protect His wife. He wants to keep her from making the kinds of bad choices that would cause her sorrow and heartache, that would drive her away from Him. But since the time of Adam and Eve, it seems that when we are given a choice between doing right or wrong, we inevitably choose wrong.

In Jeremiah, we read, "'Surely, as a wife treacherously departs from her husband, so have you dealt treacherously with Me, O house of Israel,' says the LORD" (Jeremiah 3:20). Again the prophet spoke of Israel's betrayal of her husband, writing,

Behold, the days are coming, says the LORD, when I will make a new covenant with the house of Israel and with the house of Judah—not according to the covenant that I made with their fathers in the day that I took them by the hand to lead them out of the land of Egypt, My covenant which they broke, though I was a husband to them, says the LORD (Jeremiah 31:31-32).

Ezekiel gets much more detailed in his description of the betrayal: "You trusted in your own beauty, played the harlot because of your fame, and poured out your harlotry on everyone passing by who would have it" (Ezekiel 16:15). Hosea, after being asked by God to live out a real-life example of betrayal by a prostitute wife, recorded the Lord's words:

Bring charges against your mother, bring charges; for she is not My wife, nor am I her Husband!...I will not have mercy on her children, for they are the children of harlotry. For their mother has played the harlot; she who conceived them has behaved shamefully. For she said, "I will go after my lovers, who give me my bread and my water, my wool and my linen, my oil and my drink" (Hosea 2:2,4-5).

I am writing to you as a Jew from the tribe of Judah—a born again, Spirit-filled Israeli follower of Christ. I wish I could tell you a better story of my people—paint a prettier picture of how they treated their husband. But they were utterly shameful. There was betrayal after betrayal. This heinous disregard for her wedding vows ultimately led to the dissolution of the marriage.

Thus says the LORD:
"Where is the certificate of your mother's divorce,
Whom I have put away?
Or which of My creditors is it to whom I have sold you?
For your iniquities you have sold yourselves,
And for your transgressions your mother has
been put away" (Isaiah 50:1).

Absolutely heartbreaking. Israel was chosen by the Creator God to be His beloved, but it wasn't enough. The nation exchanged the perfect for the tainted, the diseased, the sin-stricken. And she suffered the consequences. God hates divorce, but there was no other choice. He had given her chance after chance after chance, and she had thrown them all away. God said,

> Have you seen what backsliding Israel has done? She has gone up on every high mountain and under every green tree, and there played the harlot. And I said, after she had done all these things, "Return to Me." But she did not return. And her treacherous sister Judah saw it. Then I saw that for all the causes for which backsliding Israel had committed adultery, I had put her away and given her a certificate of divorce (Jeremiah 3:6-8; cf. Jeremiah 3:11-18; Ezekiel 16:35-43; Hosea 2:6-13).

There was a beautiful covenant of marriage, there was a great betrayal, there was a tragic divorce paper, and there was punishment.

But now we come to the part that so many in the Reformed tradition fail to teach. They say, "Oh, Israel was once married to God, but she betrayed Him, and God replaced her with us." If you've arrived at that conclusion, then it's evident you have only read half of your Bible. You stopped where it was convenient to you. For there is a beautiful ending to this story—this royal wedding does have a happily-ever-after.

> For Zion's sake I will not hold My peace,
> And for Jerusalem's sake I will not rest,
> Until her righteousness goes forth as brightness,
> And her salvation as a lamp that burns.
> The Gentiles shall see your righteousness,
> And all kings your glory.
> You shall be called by a new name,
> Which the mouth of the LORD will name.
> You shall also be a crown of glory
> In the hand of the LORD,
> And a royal diadem

In the hand of your God.
You shall no longer be termed Forsaken,
Nor shall your land any more be termed Desolate;
But you shall be called Hephzibah
　　["My delight is in her"], and your land Beulah
　　["Married"];
For the LORD delights in you,
And your land shall be married.
For as a young man marries a virgin,
So shall your sons marry you;
And as the bridegroom rejoices over the bride,
So shall your God rejoice over you
　　(Isaiah 62:1-5; cf. Isaiah 54:1-8; Hosea 2:14-23).

Can you feel the joy in those verses? Can you sense God's excitement at the restoration of His wife? Count the repetition of the word "shall" in this passage. Nine! "Shall" is a word that denotes a future certainty. This has not happened yet, but without a doubt it will happen in the future. And the whole world will witness and celebrate this reunion.

Ezekiel recorded this future reconciliation, penning God's promise:

> Nevertheless I will remember My covenant with you in
> the days of your youth, and I will establish an everlasting
> covenant with you…Then you shall know that I am the
> LORD, that you may remember and be ashamed, and never
> open your mouth anymore because of your shame, when
> I provide you an atonement for all you have done (Ezekiel
> 16:60,62-63).

God tells Israel that He will provide her an atonement—a *kippur.* This atonement comes in the person of Jesus. He is the One who opens the door for a new covenant based on the salvation that comes from His blood shed on the cross.

Jeremiah writes of this covenant:

> Behold, the days are coming, says the LORD, when I will
> make a new covenant with the house of Israel and with the
> house of Judah—not according to the covenant that I made

> with their fathers in the day that I took them by the hand
> to lead them out of the land of Egypt, My covenant which
> they broke, though I was a husband to them, says the LORD.
> But this is the covenant that I will make with the house of
> Israel after those days, says the LORD: I will put My law in
> their minds, and write it on their hearts; and I will be their
> God, and they shall be My people (Jeremiah 31:31-33).

How do people take this passage and make it about the church? The whole chapter is talking about God's restoration of the remnant of Israel. However, many Bible teachers will say, "But here we are talking about the new covenant. And if it's the new covenant, then it's about the church." But the Old Testament wasn't given just to the Jews and the New Testament wasn't given just to the Gentiles. God the Father is presenting His wife with a new wedding covenant. The last one was written on stone; this one will be written on her heart.

Israel was portrayed in the Scriptures as the wife of the Father, Jehovah. There was a great covenant, a great love, and a great betrayal. As a result of that betrayal, a harsh but necessary punishment was delivered. But it was a punishment with a purpose. It was discipline, not a permanent state of wrath. And at the end of their time of separation—when Jesus Christ returns to earth with His bride—there will be a restoration of the marriage of the Father to His wife, Israel, and many blessings will follow.

The Relationship Between the Son and the Church

The second intimate relationship we find in Scripture is the marriage between the Son and His bride—the church. This is not the same marital union as the one we've been looking at. There are two marriages—the Father to Israel, and the Son to the church. We must not conflate the two. This is another place where Reformed theology gets confused. it doesn't differentiate between the grooms. Those who hold to this thinking say that if Israel is called the wife of the Father and the church is called the bride of the Son and the triune God is still married to both, then doesn't that mean God is a polygamist? After all, isn't Jesus Christ also God? And because it's clear in Scripture that both Israel and the church are portrayed as wedded to God, then Israel's divorce must have been permanent and the church has become God's trophy bride.

This is completely unfounded reasoning. The Father and the Son are both the one true God, but we see throughout Scripture that they operate as their own distinct persons of the triune Godhead. So there is nothing unseemly, inappropriate, or illogical about the Father and the Son having their own spouses.

Israel is not the bride of Christ, nor is anyone else who was "declared righteous" prior to the church age. The same is true for those who will become Christians after the removal of the church at the rapture. The tribulation saints and those who will give their lives to Christ during the millennium will not be grandfathered into the church. They are of a different category. Only those who receive Jesus as their Lord and Savior during the period from Pentecost to the rapture will be part of the bride of Christ.

Paul writes to the Corinthians of the church's espousal to Christ. "I am jealous for you with godly jealousy. For I have betrothed you to one husband, that I may present you as a chaste virgin to Christ" (2 Corinthians 11:2). The betrothal is one step before marriage. The passage says, "You are already mine, but the celebration of the marriage is yet to come." The church has not become the formal bride yet, but the "save-the-date" invitations have been sent out.

To the church in Ephesus, Paul speaks of the sanctification and preparation of the bride:

> Husbands, love your wives, just as Christ also loved the church and gave Himself for her, that He might sanctify and cleanse her with the washing of water by the word, that He might present her to Himself a glorious church, not having spot or wrinkle or any such thing, but that she should be holy and without blemish (Ephesians 5:25-27).

All of us are unworthy of being wedded to the Son of God. I don't know you, but you know yourself. You don't know me, but I know myself. If we're honest, we both know how unworthy we are, don't we? Yet God is no longer looking at us through a lens that shows who we are in our shameful, naked ways. Instead, He now sees us through the filter of the blood of Jesus Christ. And that blood reveals us as having been made perfect—unsoiled and spotless because we've been washed clean by our Savior's sacrifice on the cross.

We in the church have been betrothed and prepared, and we are eagerly awaiting our marriage:

> I heard, as it were, the voice of a great multitude, as the sound of many waters and as the sound of mighty thunderings, saying, "Alleluia! For the Lord God Omnipotent reigns! Let us be glad and rejoice and give Him glory, for the marriage of the Lamb has come, and His wife has made herself ready." And to her it was granted to be arrayed in fine linen, clean and bright, for the fine linen is the righteous acts of the saints (Revelation 19:6-8).

Who are the saints? You are the saints. "Uh-oh. I know myself, Amir. I'm not a saint." Yes, you are. Remember, it's not who you are or what you've done. It's who Jesus is and what He has done for you.

The passage in Revelation continues, "Then he said to me, 'Write: "Blessed are those who are called to the marriage supper of the Lamb"!' And he said to me, 'These are the true sayings of God'" (Revelation 19:9). The Father has cleansed and prepared us for the day when we will become the bride of His Son. When will the marriage take place? Not at the time we just read about in Revelation 19. That is telling of when we return to earth with Christ at the second coming. That's not the wedding ceremony; it's the celebration afterward. It's the reception party with the fancy meal and the big cake and everybody lined up doing the Chicken Dance. The wedding itself will take place when we are raptured. The marriage won't happen here on earth, but in heaven. If you want to become the bride of Christ, then you better get yourself ready to meet your Groom in the clouds.

But the great blessings don't end there. As a good husband, Jesus is preparing an incredible eternal residence where His bride can live with Him forever. The description of this new home—the New Jeru-salem—is too long to include in this book. We will look at Revelation in detail in a few chapters. However, if you have never read about the New Jerusalem before, I would encourage you to open your Bible to Revelation 21:9-22 and prepare yourself to be amazed. As you read, remember that John is recording what we will literally experience. This is not an allegory or a parable. If you have Jesus as your Lord and Savior, you will physically walk those streets of gold and see those enormous jewels. The words in Scripture depict reality—your actual future home.

A GOD OF RESTORATION

Through Israel and the church, we learn about God. We learn that He is jealous. But He is also loving and forgiving. He is the God of res-toration and of reconciliation. While I was working on this chapter, I was thinking of all those teachers who say that God has abandoned Israel so that Israel is no longer God's people. Through this Reformed teaching that is spreading all over the world, many in the church seem to be distancing themselves from Israel—turning their backs on the nation that laid the foundation for their faith.

This made me think of the amazing story of the prodigal son. This parable can be used to illustrate the church and Israel. The faithful son can represent the church, and the prodigal can symbolize Israel. The prodigal departed to go his own way. Similarly, Israel turned its back on the Father and chased after other gods. Even when the people stopped their blatant idolatry, they exchanged one idol for another. Their love was for the law rather than for the Lawgiver. But the day will come when Israel will come back to the Lord, and He will not reject His peo-ple. Instead, like the father received the prodigal, He will embrace them and celebrate their return.

The older son, however, wanted nothing to do with the prodigal. He had remained faithful while the prodigal rejected the Savior and eventually became a secular nation. The church now sees itself as God's chosen people, not the tainted runaway.

The church should love the people of
Israel and pray for their salvation.

But why can't it be both? It's not as if God's love for Israel will take away any of His love for the church or vice versa. There's no bottom to God's love tank. If He gives much to one, there shouldn't be any concern that there will be nothing left for the other. That was the point the father was trying to make to his older son when he said, "Son, you are always with me, and all that I have is yours. It was right that we should make merry and be glad, for your brother was dead and is alive again, and was lost and is found" (Luke 15:31-32).

The church should love the people of Israel and pray for their salvation. And we should excitedly anticipate the day when the feet of Jesus will stand on the Mount of Olives with us—the saints, His bride—standing there with Him. Because it is then that Israel "will look on [Him] whom they pierced. Yes, they will mourn for Him as one mourns for his only son, and grieve for Him as one grieves for a firstborn" (Zechariah 12:10). Then out of that sorrow and recognition of the Messiah will come a nationwide repentance with every man, woman, and child falling down before their Lord and Savior. "And so all Israel will be saved" (Romans 11:26).

CHAPTER 5

GOD'S TOUGH LOVE

First to the Jew, Then to the Gentile

There is an opioid crisis that has taken hold of this world by force. In every area of the globe, drugs run rampant. Lives are being destroyed, and hundreds of thousands are dying each year. In 2017, 585,000 people died from drug use.[1] According to the United States' Centers for Disease Control and Prevention (CDC), this upward trend began in the 1990s with a marked increase in the prescribing of opioids.[2] In the 2000s, law enforcement began to crack down on illicit opioid distribution and to sanction doctors who overprescribed these dangerous medications. This made the drugs harder to come by and much more expensive.

As a result, the addicted began looking for a cheaper alternative. They found it in heroin.[3] Soon, it wasn't just junkies in urban areas who were injecting this dangerous drug, but businessmen and soccer moms and high school students out in the suburbs. Then, around 2013, a new wave of synthetic opioids began hitting the streets, including the lethal drug fentanyl.[4] Used to lace heroin, counterfeit pills, and other opioids, just a touch of the toxic substance is enough to cause a serious reaction or even death. In 2018 in the United States, 67,367 people died of drug overdoses. Just under 70 percent of those deaths were due to opioids, and, of those, two out of every three—or more than 31,000—involved the new synthetic opioids.

It is easy to look at those numbers, think *What a tragedy*, then move on. But those huge numbers are made up of individuals. It took 67,367 men and women and teens breathing their last breaths to make up that massive 2018 statistic. And for nearly all those individuals, there was a family associated. Maybe you have tragically lost members of your own family to this drug epidemic. If so, my heart breaks for you. I know that it is such a helpless feeling to watch your loved one spiral down the addiction hole.

Many do all they can to protect their addicted child or spouse or sibling as best they can. Often this leads to codependent relationships, where what feels like love can actually be what feeds the addiction. To get help, some hold interventions to try to shake their loved one out of their drug-induced craze. Others take the tough-love approach, cutting the addict off in an effort to force them to get help. I can't imagine the pain I would feel having to close the door on a child of mine who refused to get help for their dependency. But even if I were tragically forced to come to that place, I know one thing would remain true: my beloved child would never cease to be my beloved child.

A TIME OF DISCIPLINE

Israel was sin-addicted. What made it worse was that not only could the people not stop sinning, they had no desire to. They loved their sin. They relished it. It seemed that each successive generation took sin to the next level, even outdoing the sins of all the nations around them. The Lord said about the city and people of Jerusalem:

> "She has rebelled against My judgments by doing wickedness more than the nations, and against My statutes more than the countries that are all around her; for they have refused My judgments, and they have not walked in My statutes." Therefore thus says the Lord GOD: "Because you have multiplied disobedience more than the nations that are all around you, have not walked in My statutes nor

kept My judgments, nor even done according to the judgments of the nations that are all around you"—therefore
thus says the Lord GOD: "Indeed I, even I, am against you
and will execute judgments in your midst in the sight of
the nations" (Ezekiel 5:6-8).

God had sent prophet after prophet to tell the people to stop. There
was one intervention after another. Sometimes the people of Israel
and Judah would ignore the message. Other times they would angrily
kill the messenger. Still other times they would promise to change—a
promise that they might even fulfill...for a time. But ultimately, they
always ended up back in the same place, steeped in immorality and violence and greed and idol worship.

The Lord had had enough. The chances were now over. It was time
for some tough love. He told the Israelites, "I am going to bring some
very difficult times your way. And then I am going to cut you off." Just
like a parent sometimes has to cut a child off to force them to change,
God removed His hand from His children. No more blessings, no
more protection, no more listening to their prayers, no more accepting of their halfhearted worship, and no more land. He was done with
them, and they would now be on their own—broken, defeated, and
homeless. But there was one hope they still had: God's beloved children will never cease to be God's beloved children.

The prophecy we just read from Ezekiel 5 was realized when the
people of the southern kingdom of Judah were physically exiled to Babylon for seventy years. Yet there is a greater fulfillment of these words
that is seen in the spiritual exile of the Jewish people from a close relationship with God. This separation continues to this day. They rejected
the leadership of God the Father while they were in the Promised Land,
choosing instead to devote themselves to other gods.

Once the people returned to the land after their seventy-year time-
out, they once again spurned God. As we saw earlier, this time they
rejected the Son of God—Jesus the Messiah—choosing instead to
devote themselves to religion and the law. Just because something
walks like a duck and talks like a duck and prays like a duck and offers

sacrifices like a duck doesn't mean it's a duck. The Jews during the time of Christ were what Jesus called "whitewashed tombs"—they appeared "beautiful outwardly, but inside [were] full of dead men's bones and all uncleanness" (Matthew 23:27). Sadly, over the last 2,000 years, nothing has changed Israel's outside-only duckishness.

Because nothing has reformed Israel's attitude toward the Messiah, the people remain under God's tough love. But in every crisis can be found an opportunity. What is a crisis of relationship to the Jews is an opportunity for growth in the church. As the Jews continue in their discipline, the door has opened for Gentiles to discover the Messiah. That follows the pattern that God has established. Salvation was offered first to the Jew, then to the Gentile. Paul affirmed this arrangement when he said, "I am not ashamed of the gospel of Christ, for it is the power of God to salvation for everyone who believes, for the Jew first and also for the Greek" (Romans 1:16).

"But, Amir, how is that fair to the Jews for God to offer them salvation, then take that offer back and give it to the Gentiles?" It isn't that God snatched out of the Jews' hands something they desperately wanted. They weren't celebrating the Messiah and His gospel of salvation when God suddenly appeared and said, "Sorry, I'm going to need that back." Through Israel, salvation came into the world. Jesus was born a Jew and all His life He lived among His people. He opened His arms to the Jews, offering them the path to salvation through His teachings and proving His divinity through His miracles. But despite the perfection of His truth and the power of His works, the nation turned their collective back on Him. "He came to His own, and His own did not receive Him" (John 1:11).

God has His ways, and His ways are always consistent.

When Paul and Barnabas brought the gospel to Pisidian Antioch, they began in the synagogue, as was their standard procedure. Initially, there was a very positive response—a little too positive for the Jewish leaders. They became envious of Paul and Barnabas's success, so they went on the attack. When the opposition became too great, the missionaries declared, "It was necessary that the word of God should be spoken to you first; but since you reject it, and judge yourselves unworthy of everlasting life, behold, we turn to the Gentiles" (Acts 13:46). First to the Jews, then to the Gentiles.

There is order in the things of God. The world is full of chaos. Nobody and nothing can be fully depended on. But God has His ways, and His ways are always consistent. When Jesus commissioned the disciples immediately prior to returning to heaven, He said, "You shall receive power when the Holy Spirit has come upon you; and you shall be witnesses to Me in Jerusalem, and in all Judea and Samaria, and to the end of the earth" (Acts 1:8). The spread of the gospel begins in Jerusalem and Judea. First to the Jews, then to the Gentiles.

This "Jew first, Gentile second" order extends beyond the blessings of the gospel. God's judgment follows the same pattern. He will give "to those who are self-seeking and do not obey the truth, but obey unrighteousness—indignation and wrath, tribulation and anguish, on every soul of man who does evil, of the Jew first and also of the Greek" (Romans 2:8-9). Even a cursory look at the history of the Jewish people will show how they have endured "indignation and wrath, tribulation and anguish" over the last two millennia. But a day is coming soon when their tribulation will be greatly increased. It is at that time when the judgment of the Gentiles will begin. For those who are not of the church or the people of Israel, this tribulation will be a time of punishment and judgment that has no hope at the end.

For the chosen peoples, however, there is hope through this period of tribulation. After Paul promised wrath in Romans 2, he continued by saying that God will give "glory, honor, and peace to everyone who works what is good, to the Jew first and also to the Greek" (verse 10). At the end of the wrath, the people of Israel will recognize the reality of the Messiah and individually receive the gift of salvation. It is then that the Father will receive His wife back unto Himself, even as the church begins its new relationship as the bride of Christ.

AN IRREVOCABLE CALLING

Israel is in a state of tough love. When the Jews rejected the Messiah, God turned His back on them. But, remember, tough love is not a permanent severing of relationship. It is not "tough rejection" or "tough destruction." *Love* is the primary noun—*tough* is just a modifier to the subject. As Paul tells us:

> Love suffers long and is kind; love does not envy; love does not parade itself, is not puffed up; does not behave rudely, does not seek its own, is not provoked, thinks no evil; does not rejoice in iniquity, but rejoices in the truth; bears all things, believes all things, hopes all things, endures all things. Love never fails (1 Corinthians 13:4-8).

These characteristics describe God, because "God is love" (1 John 4:8). And just as God's love never fails to His chosen people of the church, so will His love never fail to His chosen people of Israel. So rather than writing the Jews off as has-beens in the plan of God, the church should be celebrating them. It is because the gospel was offered to the Jews that the Gentiles can now receive it, according to the order that God has established. "I say then, have they stumbled that they should fall? Certainly not! But through their fall, to provoke them to jealousy, salvation has come to the Gentiles" (Romans 11:11). First to the Jew, then to the Gentile.

In fact, to disregard the Jews as having fallen too far away for redemption is the height of hypocrisy.

> Concerning the gospel [the Jews] are enemies for your sake, but concerning the election they are beloved for the sake of the fathers. For the gifts and the calling of God are irrevocable. For as you were once disobedient to God, yet have now obtained mercy through their disobedience, even so these also have now been disobedient, that through the mercy shown you they also may obtain mercy. For God has committed them all to disobedience, that He might have mercy on all (Romans 11:28-32).

First, Paul says that the gifts and calling of God are irrevocable. If you are called by God, then you will always be called by Him. Aren't you thankful that is true? If there were some arbitrary level of sinfulness that, when passed, would revoke God's gift of eternal life, how could anyone have peace? You would always be wondering which side of the line you are on. Has my sin meter reached the level that my ejection seat will be triggered and I will be jettisoned from the elect to the discarded?

The other purpose Paul has in this Romans 11 passage is to correct some selective memory amongst those in the church. Who were you before Christ? A sinner. What changed that? God's mercy. Did you deserve it? No. Well, then, how are the Jews any different? In fact, just like their disobedience had a hand in you repenting and receiving mercy, so your obedience can now have a hand in their repentance and receiving mercy. How incredible is that!

The gifts and calling of God are irrevocable. If you are called by God, then you will always be called by Him.

God has not rejected Israel. In fact, He has already begun to set the stage for when He calls them out of their tough-love exile and invites them back home. How do we know? We listen closely for the sound of Him calling them back home.

BY THE POWER OF SAN REMO

A special centennial celebration took place in April 2020. It was the one-hundredth anniversary of the San Remo Conference of April 20-26, 1920—an event that, if people had listened closely, they would have heard the sound of God calling His chosen people back to Himself. To understand the significance of San Remo, we need to go back a few years earlier to the end of World War I.

In 1917, former British prime minister Lord Arthur Balfour was Britain's foreign minister. While serving in that capacity, he wrote a letter to Lord Rothschild, who was the head of a Jewish banking family and a supporter of Zionism.

> Foreign Office
> November 2nd, 1917
>
> Dear Lord Rothschild,
>
> I have much pleasure in conveying to you, on behalf of His Majesty's Government, the following declaration of sympathy with Jewish Zionist aspirations which has been submitted to, and approved by, the Cabinet.
>
>> "His Majesty's Government view with favour the establishment in Palestine of a national home for the Jewish people, and will use their best endeavours to facilitate the achievement of this object, it being clearly understood that nothing shall be done which may prejudice the civil and religious rights of existing non-Jewish communities in Palestine, or the rights and political status enjoyed by Jews in any other country."
>
> I should be grateful if you would bring this declaration to the knowledge of the Zionist Federation.
>
> Yours sincerely,
> Arthur James Balfour[5]

This was a noteworthy letter because it was the first time that any government had pledged their support to the formation of a Jewish national home. And not only a home, but one in the land that had been given to the Jews by God so long ago. The borders of this land—at that time referred to as Palestine—were very different than how they are drawn today. If you were to look at a map of that time, you would see that this formerly Ottoman territory included not just what is now Israel but also Jordan. So, when this letter was sent, Balfour and the Cabinet were not considering separate states of Palestine and Jordan. The country of Jordan was formed later, then it was offered as a gift to the Hashemites—a Bedouin tribe from Arabia—out of gratitude for their help to the British army in World War I. But in 1917, the British government urged the entire territory encompassing modern-day Israel and Jordan to be considered for the national homeland for the Jewish people.

While the Balfour Declaration was a great first step, it had no legal authority. It was simply a nice pronouncement presented by the British on behalf of the Jews. It was at the April 1920 San Remo conference that this sentiment developed some teeth. Attending this gathering were Great Britain, Italy, France, and Japan, with the United States along as a neutral observer. This summit continued discussions between these nations that had begun in London two months earlier. Their purpose was to determine what to do with captured territories from the First World War.

The attending international powers decided it was best to put Palestine under British Mandatory rule. These powers also agreed to the following:

> The Mandatory will be responsible for putting into effect the declaration originally made on November 8, 1917, by the British government, and adopted by the other Allied Powers, in favour of the establishment in Palestine of a national home for the Jewish people, it being clearly understood that nothing shall be done which may prejudice the civil and religious rights of existing non-Jewish communities in Palestine, or the rights and political status enjoyed by Jews in any other country.[6]

Are you grasping the significance of this? The British were nice enough to give a declaration, but at San Remo the declaration became an abiding international agreement. This is the legal basis for Israel to be in its land and for the boundaries to be as they were originally intended—including both modern-day Israel and Jordan.

Those original borders didn't last long. Soon, the British decided they preferred the crude oil of the Arabs to the olive oil of the Jews, so they began chipping off territories from the map. They cut off two-thirds to become Transjordan, and gave it to the Hashemites. They cut off the Golan Heights and gave it to the French in a territorial exchange. All the while, the agreed-to 1920 borders shrank more and more. Then came the November 1947 United Nations resolution that recommended the partition of Palestine—an action this body did not have the authority to take, but would have enforced had not a civil war broken out that eventually led to the establishment of the State of Israel.

That is why we celebrate the April 1920 San Remo resolution and why its centennial was such a special event. It was at San Remo that Israel was essentially planned and established. Then it took us twenty-eight years and a bloody war to declare and formalize our independence.

THE TIME IS COMING SOON

"Interesting history lesson, Amir. Is there a point?" Fair, but a somewhat snarky question. Bear with me a little longer. Many believers confuse the trumpets of Revelation—the seven trumpets that usher in seven judgments found in chapters 8–11—with the trumpet that we will hear before the rapture and the trumpet that will announce the second coming of Jesus. That's understandable. There are a lot of trumpets in the Bible. But as we saw back in chapter 2, not every trumpet in the Bible automatically points to Revelation. Trumpets were part of the Jewish culture and their soundings were anything but a rare occurrence.

While excavating along the Western Wall of the Temple Mount in Jerusalem, an interesting find was made. A large, L-shaped stone pushed down during the Roman destruction of the Temple was found with an incomplete Hebrew inscription that read "To the house of trumpeting to announce..."[7] What was this trumpeting and what was it announcing? The answers are found in the priests' desire to ensure that no one forgot about or was late for religious events. From this corner of the Temple wall, a trumpet would be sounded at intervals to let the Jewish people know that the Sabbath was about to begin or that the holidays were ready to commence.

The first blowing of the trumpet was to bring closer those who were still far away.

The second blowing of the trumpet was to bring closer to the city those who were halfway home.

The third blast was to let those who were busy immediately outside of the city walls know that it was time to start heading in.

The fourth was to warn those at the city gates that they should begin entering.

The fifth was to encourage those on the streets of the city to start walking to their houses.

The sixth was to let those already in their homes know that it was time to start preparing for the Sabbath.

The seventh was let everyone know that the time had come—the beginning of the Sabbath or the holiday had arrived.

Each of these trumpet soundings was a reminder to the people that the time was coming soon. Prepare now. Don't wait until the last minute. You don't want the Sabbath to start while you're still outside the city or running home on empty streets. I believe that over the past 100 years or so, these trumpets have been sounding the coming commencement of a great event.

The Balfour Declaration was a blowing of the trumpet. "I'm bringing My people home like I said I would."

The San Remo convention was a blowing of the trumpet. "I've established the borders of the land where My nation will gather, just like I promised they would before My return." These are signs that the reward for the church is near and the end of Israel's period of tough love is drawing nigh.

There have been other trumpets too. The Holocaust was a loud trumpet calling the Jews back to their land. The day of Israel's independence in 1948, the God-aided victory in the 1967 Six-Day War, the miraculous success of the 1973 Yom Kippur War, the growth in the population, economy, and power of the State of Israel, the 2018 recognition by President Donald Trump that Jerusalem is Israel's capital city—these are all trumpets saying, "Hurry. Prepare. The day is soon." They are not just historical events. They are God's way of getting our attention so that we are ready for what is next.

What specifically are these trumpet blasts announcing? They are proclaiming the completion of Ezekiel 36–37. God promised,

> You, O mountains of Israel, you shall shoot forth your branches and yield your fruit to My people Israel, for they are about to come. For indeed I am for you, and I will turn to you, and you shall be tilled and sown. I will multiply men upon you, all the house of Israel, all of it; and the cities shall be inhabited and the ruins rebuilt. I will multiply upon you man and beast; and they shall increase and bear young; I will make you inhabited as in former times, and do better for you than at your beginnings. Then you shall know that I am the LORD (Ezekiel 36:8-11).

Again, He vowed,

> Surely I will take the children of Israel from among the nations, wherever they have gone, and will gather them from every side and bring them into their own land; and I will make them one nation in the land, on the mountains of Israel; and one king shall be king over them all; they shall no longer be two nations, nor shall they ever be divided into two kingdoms again (Ezekiel 37:21-22).

To a nineteenth-century Bible reader, these events would have seemed inconceivable. A national State of Israel? Ridiculous. A gathering of the thousands of Jewish enclaves around the world into one land? Impossible.

Then the trumpets started blaring. In 1917 and 1920 and 1948 and on up to today, they resounded, saying, "Get ready, because once chapters 36 and 37 of Ezekiel are done, 38 and 39 will come. And you don't want to be here for 38 and 39." The former two chapters relate the restoration of the land and the gathering of God's people into one place. Once that is done, the Lord will begin the discipline of the nations related in the latter two chapters. This discipline is the great tribulation, or "the time of Jacob's trouble" (Jeremiah 30:7). This is when we see the events of Revelation take place, which we will examine in chapters

7–11 of this book. This will be a time of global devastation greater than anything previously seen.

ARE YOU LISTENING?

How do you feel as you think about these trumpets sounding? Do they make you nervous, or do you experience a growing sense of excitement? Are you fearful of the coming wrath, or do you feel peaceful in the hope of Jesus' return? Your answers to those questions will largely depend on where you are with the Savior. Every sound of the trumpet brings the world one step closer to the great tribulation. But it also brings every Christian one step closer to seeing Jesus' face.

Those of us who have given our lives to Jesus and received His forgiveness will not be part of the horrors of the tribulation. We are not destined for wrath. Jesus promised for those who "have kept My command to persevere, I also will keep you from the hour of trial which shall come upon the whole world, to test those who dwell on the earth" (Revelation 3:10). According to Jesus' words, for us to avoid the trial that will come upon the whole earth, we must no longer be of those who dwell on the earth. There are three options for no longer being earth-dwellers—we will be dead, we will be removed, or we will be living in a biosphere on Mars. Since Mars has not yet been colonized, it really comes down to the first two possibilities—death or removal.

For the members of the church to be snatched from the earth, a supernatural act needs to take place. This can only happen by the hand of God:

> For the Lord Himself will descend from heaven with a shout, with the voice of an archangel, and with the trumpet of God. And the dead in Christ will rise first. Then we who are alive and remain shall be caught up together with them in the clouds to meet the Lord in the air. And thus we shall always be with the Lord. Therefore comfort one another with these words (1 Thessalonians 4:16-18).

That promise of being gone during the tribulation is our comfort as we see those seven years approaching. You don't encourage each other by saying, "Hey, let's meet up so we can go through the tribulation together. All that death and destruction going on—it'll be a hoot."

In the church, our eyes are fixed on what God is doing with Israel so that we can get an idea of how soon our gathering is going to be. That is why it is so important to be scanning the news, listening for the trumpets. You'll hear their sound when you listen to what God is doing in Israel. Even in the midst of the wars and rumors of wars, Israel is still strong. Even through the coronavirus, we're still the most powerful nation in the Middle East.

In the church, our eyes are fixed on what God is doing with Israel so that we can get an idea of how soon our gathering is going to be.

In the coronavirus, we can also see the way the enemy continues to attack. Because of how well Israel fared at first, some believed that we had discovered a cure and were not sharing it with the world. That was baloney, of course, but you can't fight against such people. Our lack of a cure became very evident when Israel was later forced to lock back down due to a second outbreak. Still, anti-Semitism continues to grow around the globe. A whole new brand of hatred against Israel has been growing in the church through the internet conspiracy rantings of various false prophets blaming "Zionism" for everything from wars to riots to the pandemic. The worst part about this ridiculous garbage is that they claim the Bible as their foundation, using shoddy hermeneutics and preconceived conclusions. How the Holy Spirit must shake His head at such a heretical handling of His inspired Word.

For those who have a rosy optimism about the future of our planet, I've got bad news. This world is not going to get better. It is not going

to suddenly become wonderful with enemies reconciling and wars ending and pollution disappearing and the polar bears regaining all their
lost icy real estate. Life is not going to get safer and easier. Jesus said, "I
go to prepare a place for you. And if I go and prepare a place for you, I
will come again and receive you to Myself; that where I am, there you
may be also" (John 14:2-3). He is coming so that we can be there with
Him, not so that He can dwell here with us. He is preparing our future
home, not expecting us to prepare His future home. It is this promise
that will give those of us in the church peace and enable us to encourage one another.

If the people of Israel were to hear the trumpets and understand
their true meaning, they would not feel that same peace. There is no
short-term encouragement for Jews who have not made Jesus their
Savior. They are taking a path separate from the church, and they will
remain earthbound through the coming time of trouble. Yet there is
still hope long-term. Remember, God the Father will never be done
with His sin-addicted children. Their period of tough love will come
to an end. Once the fullness of the Gentiles has come in and the time
of tribulational discipline has reached its completion, in that glorious
day, "all Israel will be saved" (Romans 11:26). If there is any solace for
the people of Israel, it will be found in that.

CHAPTER 6

GOD'S APPOINTED TIMES

*Understanding Time So We
Can Understand the Times*

I t's hard to imagine a time without time. Time just is—like air. You
don't think about it, you just live it. Time is a constant. On the other
hand, time is anything but constant. Despite being constantly with us,
time is constantly moving away from us. It may be the least constant
of this universe. Each moment of time lasts a nanosecond, then moves
to the next. Yet we are never without time. Even when God made the
sun stand still for Joshua and his army, the Bible says, "The sun stood
still in the midst of heaven, and did not hasten to go down for about a
whole day" (Joshua 10:13). The sun may have stopped, but the minutes
and hours continued until almost a whole day had passed.

We cannot escape the passing of time. The older we get, the more
evident this truth is. But even though time always is, it hasn't always
been. There was a time when there was no time. Before God created
all things, He lived in a time without time. There were no seconds
or minutes or hours or days. He wouldn't wake up in the morning
and wonder how He was going to spend His day because there was
no morning and there was no day. Time is a wonderful result of His

creation—something that allows us to discern the past from the present from the future. But time is not necessary. God is not bound by time. Jesus demonstrated His existence outside of the normal understanding of time when, ignoring the grammar necessitated by the passing of time, He said to the Pharisees, "Most assuredly, I say to you, before Abraham was, I AM" (John 8:58). A powerful affirmation of His deity that is sure to make most English teachers cringe.

This existence before time is a God-only experience. Contrary to certain belief systems, we were not living with Him as spirit babies in a pre-earthborn state. However, even though we did not exist with Him before time began, we will be with Him when time is no more—if we have received Jesus as our Lord and Savior. God has already appointed when time will end, and, if He has appointed it, we can be absolutely sure that it will come to pass.

For now, it often feels like time runs our lives. We have our appointments and our schedules. We know where we need to be and when we need to be there. If someone is punctual about showing up for meetings, we see that as a sign of good character. If someone is late, we feel disrespected and wonder if that person can be depended on in other areas of life. Time tells us when to go to bed and when to wake up. It sets the moment we need to be at work or when we have to drive the kids to soccer practice or when we must arrive at church so that we can be sure to get our usual seats.

It is this dependence on time that has so many believers sitting at home with a stopwatch, thinking, *Okay, God, when is the rapture going to happen? You said soon, and by this point You're probably stretching the outer limits of even the most liberal definitions of that word. A day or even a week, that can still fit the "soon" definition. But two thousand years feels a little excessive.* So Christians make predictions and set dates. But, as tough as it is for us to accept, when we ask God, "When?," His answer is typically, "None of your business."

The prophet Habakkuk once threw God a "When?" question, to which the Lord replied, "The vision is yet for an appointed time; but at the end it will speak, and it will not lie. Though it tarries, wait for it; because it will surely come, it will not tarry" (Habakkuk 2:3). God told

Habakkuk that He has appointed a time when all the prophet's concerns will be addressed. But that time is not now. There is no reason to be impatient. While it may feel to Habakkuk like time is dragging on, to God, the timing is perfect.

This is the same message God gives to us as we long for His return. It is a good thing to desire the return of Christ. However, if you think He is tarrying, it is because of your own impatience. He has appointed a time, and that time will surely come because He who promised is faithful. This is true of all aspects of God's plan for this world. He has appointed times, and He has the authority to determine when and how His plan will be carried out.

In order to understand the distinctions between Israel and the church, we must pay attention to their individual timelines. Both run separate courses through the histories and futures that the Lord has laid out. But to recognize how these two paths intersect and diverge, we need to appreciate the concept of time and how God uses it to carry out His will. This is particularly true when we look at the end of all time as laid out in the book of Revelation. So, before we begin examining that wonderful apocalyptic book written by the apostle John, we need to establish a framework as to how God works both inside and outside of time.

THE ETERNAL GOD CREATED TIME
WHEN HE CREATED THE WORLD

"In the beginning…" (Genesis 1:1). It is in the first three words of the Bible that time is introduced. The fact there is a beginning implies that there is also a middle and an end. Time passes from *a* to *b* until finally arriving at *c*. Whose hand is behind this creation? Of course, it is the Father's through His Son, the Word. "In the beginning was the Word, and the Word was with God, and the Word was God. He was in the beginning with God. All things were made through Him, and without Him nothing was made that was made" (John 1:1-3). Jesus "made," and time was the natural by-product.

From those first acts of creation, God began defining times. First, He gave us days. "Then God said, 'Let there be light'; and there was light.

And God saw the light, that it was good; and God divided the light from the darkness. God called the light Day, and the darkness He called Night. So the evening and the morning were the first day" (Genesis 1:3-5). Sundown, then sunup—you've got yourself a day. This was the first time that there was a First Day. You call it Sunday, but in Hebrew we call it First Day. Why? Because it's the first day of the week. Sunday may not always be sunny, but there is never a week when First Day is not first.

Months were established by God. As He informed Moses and Aaron of His plan to destroy the firstborn of all Egypt, He said, "This month shall be your beginning of months; it shall be the first month of the year to you" (Exodus 12:2). Passover instituted the Jewish months, and a series of months became a year.

Seasons were also ordained by God. After the flood, the Lord smelled the wonderful aroma of Noah's sacrifice and made the promise, "While the earth remains, seedtime and harvest, cold and heat, winter and summer, and day and night shall not cease" (Genesis 8:22). God created global warming. He also created global cooling. There will be hot times and cold times, planting times and reaping times—each in their proper season.

When God created, time began. He then took time and arranged it in an orderly fashion so that we could mark its passing. This is the system that now directs our days.

GOD CREATED US WITHIN TIME

When God spoke forth mankind's "Let Us make…" moment, it was within time. Five days had already passed since He had begun the creation process. In that moment, we were inserted into the flow of history. Why then and not before? Because all creation before that point had been in preparation for this crowning achievement of His creative plan. This was the glorious instant when He inserted part of Himself into His creation—the implanting of the supernatural into the natural, the spiritual into the physical. "'Let Us make man in Our image, according to Our likeness…' So God created man in His own image; in the image of God He created him; male and female He created them" (Genesis 1:26-27). From that first instant of human history, we have been following God's established plan, governed by His times and moments and seasons.

Jesus, during His earthly ministry, was Himself governed by the Father's times. While walking with His disciples, He told them, "My time has not yet come, but your time is always ready" (John 7:6). Similarly, when His own mother asked Him to help out at the wedding in Cana, Jesus' response was, "My hour has not yet come" (John 2:4). The Father had established the times of His Son, and His Son was subject to them.

God has ordered our times. We may feel like our time is our own, but it actually belongs to Him. "My times are in Your hand; deliver me from the hand of my enemies, and from those who persecute me" (Psalm 31:15). You don't have ultimate control over your days. You may have your life all planned out—your educational plans, your career path, when you want to marry, when to start a family, the age of your retirement, and how much money you will have put away so that you can enjoy the remainder of your years. That's all great. But you also need to recognize that at any given point you might walk in front of a truck or be stricken with a debilitating disease or discover your inability to have children or get derailed from your career.

Paul wrote, "See then that you walk circumspectly, not as fools but as wise, redeeming the time, because the days are evil" (Ephesians 5:15-16; cf. Colossians 4:5). God, who sits outside of time, sees all our days. He has established the beginning and the end, and He knows all the bumps and bruises we'll face along the way. He says, "Plan for the future, but make the most of now. Today is here; you can't be sure about tomorrow. Be sure you are shining My light every moment of every day while you still have time."

OUR SOVEREIGN GOD HAS DETERMINED THE WHAT, WHEN, AND WHERE OF ALL THINGS

One of life's more helpless feelings comes in that moment when you realize that the pen you have been using to write on a whiteboard is filled with permanent ink. There's no going back. You can wipe, you can spray, you can plead with the whiteboard angels to come and rescue you, but the reality remains that the dark smudges that now mar the once-pristine surface will never fully go away.

God's plans are perfect; therefore,
His set times are perfect.

Our God is sovereign, which means that He is the one in control of all things. As sovereign, He not only has the authority to establish all times, but the power to carry out those times. His plans are perfect; therefore, His set times are perfect. God's sovereignty means that if He had a giant whiteboard calendar on which He was going to fill in all the important moments of history, He could do so using a Sharpie. No circumstances would have Him reaching for the eraser. No crises, such as wars or viruses or natural disasters, would have Him googling "permanent ink solvents." What He has established is 100 percent perfection and will come to pass.

The Perfect Moment for Creation

God determined the perfect moment for the world's creation. In His existence outside of time, God chose the perfect time to start time. Stephen Hawking couldn't figure out why this universe appeared when it did. His book *A Brief History of Time* gave no insight as to how time became time. Instead, he gave his suppositions about the whens and the hows of the universe, yet offered no answers for the philosophical question of why. But the solution really isn't difficult. The universe happened because God decided it would happen. It happened when it did for the same reason—the Lord decided it was right.

The Perfect Moment for the Flood

God determined the perfect moment for sending a flood upon the world. One day, our sovereign Lord pulled Noah aside and revealed to him when He would send the flood and how long it would last. He didn't say, "Hey, Noah, I was thinking about flooding the earth. Let Me know how long you think it would take you to build an ark so I can map out a timeline." The Lord didn't check in every now and again on his boatbuilder—"You getting any closer? I'm trying to nail down this schedule." God had His times already established, and when the ark was done, He told his faithful servant, "Come into the ark, you and all your household, because I have seen that you are righteous before Me in this generation…For after seven more days I will cause it to rain on the earth forty days and forty nights, and I will destroy from the face of the earth all living things that I have made" (Genesis 7:1,4). He gave his servant a date for the flood—one week from that day—and Noah had to live with that reality for the next seven days.

Imagine looking around you with the knowledge that every person you saw, with the exception of your immediate family, would be dead in a week's time. What would you do with those seven days? We know what Noah did—he told everyone to get straight with God while there was still time. The apostle Peter called Noah a "preacher of righteousness" (2 Peter 2:5), and we have to assume that is exactly what he was doing as he watched the timer tick down to zero.

When God wants us to know a date, He'll tell us the date. And if He keeps that knowledge from us, there is always a reason. Every person on this earth has a countdown clock on their lives. We were born with an expiration date. Noah knew what his contemporaries' timers were set at—we don't have such knowledge today. That lack of certainty should be a fire set under us to also be preachers of righteousness, because our unbelieving friends and family may have seventy years, or seven days, or maybe just until tomorrow.

The Perfect Moment for Abraham's Son

God determined the perfect moment when He would fulfill His

promise to Abraham to give him a son. In the covenant God made with Abraham, the Lord told him that He would "make [him] a great nation" (Genesis 12:2). That had to have thrilled this old man who had likely given up all hope of having children. Then time went on without any offspring, and he started wondering if maybe God had forgotten His promise. Eventually his patience ran out, so he thought he would give God a hand by having a child through his wife's servant, Hagar. This one act of impatience has led to 4,000 years of enmity between Hagar's son, Ishmael, and Sarah's soon-to-come son, Isaac.

If only we would learn to wait on God—to trust that He already has the time of our prayer's answer written on His whiteboard in permanent ink. Abraham's answer was on that board in big, bold letters, and had been for ages. Knowing Abraham's desperation, one day God decided to give this future patriarch a glimpse at His calendar. He and two angels visited Abraham. While there, He told the father of His chosen people, "At the appointed time I will return to you, according to the time of life, and Sarah shall have a son" (Genesis 18:14). God had appointed a time. And when Abraham appointed his own time, he created a mess.

When the Lord's appointed time came to pass—boom!—there was a son born to this aged couple. Through this son, Isaac, God's chosen people would descend. Israel was established at just the right moment, according to God's calendar. The descendants of this miracle child would be blessings to the whole world, and through this line would one day come the Savior of mankind. Thus, Abraham became a father twice over. He became the physical father of the Jews, and he became the spiritual father of the church and ultimately of all those whose salvation is found in Jesus Christ. One father, one promised child, two separate and very distinct lines of descendants.

The Perfect Moment for Jesus' Birth

God determined the perfect moment for His Son to come into the world. Before time began, God had written the arrival of Immanuel onto His calendar. "[Christ] indeed was foreordained before the foundation of the world, but was manifest in these last times for you who through Him believe in God, who raised Him from the dead and gave Him glory, so that your faith and hope are in God" (1 Peter 1:20-21). When the time arrived, Jesus, *Yeshua HaMashiach*—the salvation of the world—was born in a small town just south of Jerusalem. "When the fullness of the time had come, God sent forth His Son, born of a woman, born under the law, to redeem those who were under the law, that we might receive the adoption as sons" (Galatians 4:4-5).

There was a set time, a set day, a set hour that Jesus had to come. Why did He come then and not at another point in history? We can speculate all we want and come up with some very logical conclusions. But ultimately, the timing was perfect because the Father determined it to be perfect. The very second that our Savior took His first humble breath down amongst His creation had been determined before the universe had even been formed. Again, God's perfect timing is not based on events or circumstances. It is perfect because it is God's timing.

The Perfect Moment for Jesus' Ministry

God determined the perfect moment for the beginning of Jesus' ministry. Mark writes, "Now after John was put in prison, Jesus came to Galilee, preaching the gospel of the kingdom of God, and saying, 'The time is fulfilled, and the kingdom of God is at hand. Repent, and believe in the gospel'" (Mark 1:14-15). Luke 3:23 says that Jesus was about thirty years old when He started His ministry. Think about what it would have been like if He had started His ministry at age twenty-one. Or even if He was recognized as a child prodigy and began to heal people and spread the gospel at age thirteen. Couldn't He have cast out so many more demons and healed so many more lepers and given sight to so many more blind people and preached the gospel of salvation to so many more lost? God became man and lived on this earth for just thirty-three years, and only 9 percent of those years were spent in ministry. Wasn't that a waste? Absolutely not. The length of His ministry was perfect. Why? Because God set the time.

The Perfect Moment for Jesus' Crucifixion

God determined the perfect moment for His Son to die. Having just typed those words, I admit that I have to pause as I consider this. The Father Himself planned out the agonizing sacrifice of His only Son. I can't imagine it. Outside of God Himself, there is no one I love more than my family. You may be a wonderful person, but if it came to me making a choice between you and one of them? Sorry, my family will win every time. I would readily sacrifice myself for you, but keep your hands off my wife and children. Yet the Father's love for us was so great that He willingly traded His Son's life for ours. Take a moment before reading on, and think about what God has done for you and thank Him for it.

When Jesus sent the disciples to prepare the Passover the night before His crucifixion, He revealed to them that "My time is at hand" (Matthew 26:18). The timer on Jesus' death had started the moment He was born, and the buzzer was about to go off. "When we were still without strength, in due time Christ died for the ungodly" (Romans 5:6). He had lived His life with the specter of crucifixion hanging over His head, and now it was "due time." Imagine living your life with the knowledge that on a certain day you would die a horrific death. Every morning you would wake up recognizing that you were twenty-four hours closer to the end. A year away, a month away, a day away—it's no wonder Jesus' anguish was so great at Gethsemane. But the time had come; it had to be done. Thus, we see Jesus' acquiescence to the time set by the Father—"Not My will, but Yours, be done" (Luke 22:42).

The Perfect Moment for Sending the Spirit

God determined the perfect moment to send the Holy Spirit to birth the church. The night before Jesus went to the cross, He talked to His disciples about the Spirit that was to come to them. "When the Helper comes, whom I shall send to you from the Father, the Spirit of truth who proceeds from the Father, He will testify of Me" (John 15:26). In those times to come when they would begin doubting what Jesus had said about Himself, the Holy Spirit would be there to deal with the disbelief and to affirm what they knew to be true.

The Spirit's ministry of wisdom would extend beyond just the words of Jesus to all truth. In that same conversation, Jesus went on to say,

> Nevertheless I tell you the truth. It is to your advantage that I go away; for if I do not go away, the Helper will not come to you; but if I depart, I will send Him to you... When He, the Spirit of truth, has come, He will guide you into all truth; for He will not speak on His own authority, but whatever He hears He will speak; and He will tell you things to come. He will glorify Me, for He will take of what is Mine and declare it to you (John 16:7,13-14).

Why did the Holy Spirit have to wait until after the death of Jesus to begin this wonderful ministry of truth and affirmation? Because the Father had determined it to be best.

Every important event on the world's spiritual calendar
has been set through the wisdom and sovereignty of God,
and every one will come to pass at just the right moment.

The Perfect Moments for Future Events

Finally, through the church age and the times to come, God's schedule is set. He has determined the perfect moment that Jesus will come and redeem the church from the coming wrath (Matthew 24:36; 1 Thessalonians 1:9-10). He has set the date when He will reward His saints for their deeds with a crown of righteousness (2 Timothy 4:8; cf. Colossians 3:23-24). He has decided the glorious period when Israel will experience revival and return to Him (Romans 11:26). He has fixed the timing for that great day when He will send His Son with the Son's bride to rule and judge the world (Revelation 19:4-21; cf. Acts 17:30-31). Finally, the Lord has fixed just the right moments for Him to bring all humanity to a final judgment (Revelation 20:12) and to establish

His new heavens and new earth (Revelation 21:1-4). Every important event on the world's spiritual calendar has been set through the wisdom and sovereignty of God, and every one will come to pass at just the right moment.

THE HOLY SPIRIT GIVES
US THE ABILITY TO
UNDERSTAND GOD'S TIMES

There are some people who have a remarkable ability to recognize trends and make reasonably accurate political, cultural, and spiritual prognostications. Depending on how well these men and women are able to communicate their predictions—or how many books they manage to sell—they can even have an influence on the course that nations take. This is not a new phenomenon. When David was in Hebron, amassing men for the inevitable conflict with Ish-bosheth, the son of the late King Saul, among those listed were "the sons of Issachar who had understanding of the times, to know what Israel ought to do" (1 Chronicles 12:32). These men had a godly wisdom that allowed them to see that the time had come for God to shift the power in Israel from the line of a spiritually failed king to a new king, one who would be a man after God's own heart.

Today, the world is living in a time that is more difficult to understand than usual. In the United States, protests and riots and lootings have taken place. People are calling for police departments to be defunded. There is an intentional movement to erase history through the removal of statuary and the "cancelling" of various books, movies, and music that have been deemed "hateful" by a small but powerful multigenerational and multiethnic minority of the populace. Those who have any sort of public prominence are forced to kowtow to the socialist political organization Black Lives Matter (BLM) or face mobs, loss of position, and sometimes violence. What started as a movement to address lingering racism in various parts of the American culture has been hijacked by those with an extreme left-wing agenda and is now being used to fundamentally overhaul American government and culture.

Churches—still reeling from being locked shut for months due to

COVID—are wrestling with how to deal with the BLM movement. Many prominent Christian leaders are mistakenly kneeling in repentance before members of the African American community, saying they accept responsibility for "white privilege" and the nation's racist past. Others stand adamantly opposed to such demonstrations, saying, "I will only bend my knee to Jesus Christ." Most Christians find themselves confused as to how they should respond—praying that any lingering systemic racism be properly dealt with, but wondering how repenting for sins they never committed will do anything except give more strength to a radical movement that they fundamentally distrust.

The confusion about what is taking place is real, but not necessary. God has offered us wisdom to understand our times, if we will just ask. The Holy Spirit will guide our actions as we seek His will. Only through the Spirit can the murky waters of culture truly be cleared so that we can see the path we're called to walk in these strange and unusual times. And with the Holy Spirit, there is not always a one-size-fits-all direction. God's plans and purposes are far too big for that. So, while kneeling in the name of reconciliation may be the wrong response for some people, it may be just what is needed for others in order to further a wider plan that God has put into action. Because of this, Christians must be slow to judge other Christians when it comes to actions and reactions that are not clearly delineated as moral or immoral in Scripture.

In the same way that the Holy Spirit can bring clarity to our current situation, He can open our eyes toward understanding future times. The Father has already revealed to us many of the events that are coming our way, and He has done this through the prophets. The shepherd prophet, Amos, wrote, "Surely the Lord God does nothing, unless He reveals His secret to His servants the prophets" (Amos 3:7). The message comes to the prophets, and the prophets pass it on to the people. They are the heralds of the Word of the Lord. Therefore, their words can be taken as absolute truth. "No prophecy of Scripture is of any private interpretation, for prophecy never came by the will of man, but holy men of God spoke as they were moved by the Holy Spirit" (2 Peter 1:20-21).

The prophets in Scripture spoke words directly from the mouth of God. That is why I will never claim to be a prophet. Today it seems that everyone wants to be a prophet. Pastors and evangelists—in order to bolster their authority and reputation—call themselves Prophet Joe or Prophet Bill. Or, if you can add a Jewish name to your title, it's just that much stronger. "I am now Prophet Yehuda ben Israel," a pastor might announce to his congregation, while his wife is busy in his office shredding all his old business cards that read "Pastor Bucky Johnson."

On one occasion I met a lady on the jetway into an airplane. She said, "Oh my! You're Prophet Amir!" I almost had a heart attack. I am not a conduit for God's holy words. I don't have a scribe copying down my pronouncements so that I can add First and Second Amir as the sixty-seventh and sixty-eighth books of the Bible. What I teach are the insights that the Holy Spirit gives to me *from* the inspired Word of God. Those same insights are available to all who will take the time to study the Scriptures.

Therefore, it is the Holy Spirit who, through the Bible, has blessed us with information regarding the Father's timing for both Israel and the church. And it is the Holy Spirit who then gives us insight into that information through our times of reading and studying His Word. But there is a limit to what He will show us. Many of us, by nature, are inquisitive. We want answers, and we want them now. Wanting answers is not a bad thing. In fact, we should desire to know all we can know about God and His plans. However, we must also realize that there is a lot of information that is just plain above our pay grade. God hasn't revealed it to us for a reason.

Before Jesus ascended into heaven, the disciples questioned Him:

> "Lord, will You at this time restore the kingdom to Israel?" And He said to them, "It is not for you to know times or seasons which the Father has put in His own authority. But you shall receive power when the Holy Spirit has come upon you; and you shall be witnesses to Me in Jerusalem, and in all Judea and Samaria, and to the end of the earth" (Acts 1:6-8).

The disciples asked a great question. Jesus replied, "Sorry, I can't give you an answer. Instead, I'll give you a mission. You focus on your work here, and let the Father deal with the times."

Be satisfied with what you can know through the wisdom and insight of the Holy Spirit. At the same time, beware of those who promise secret knowledge and who delve into matters not clearly spelled out in Scripture. Peter warned against these sorts of false teachers in his second letter:

> These [false teachers] are wells without water, clouds carried by a tempest, for whom is reserved the blackness of darkness forever. For when they speak great swelling words of emptiness, they allure through the lusts of the flesh, through lewdness, the ones who have actually escaped from those who live in error. While they promise them liberty, they themselves are slaves of corruption (2 Peter 2:17-19).

These false teachers are "wells without water," offering insights that they claim will sate the curiosity of those wanting to see behind the doors of knowledge that God has intentionally kept shut. Sadly, many buy into these promises and spend all their time dropping their buckets into an empty well, ignoring the overflowing, life-giving water contained in the Bible. Jesus said, "It is not for you to know the times or seasons," but the false prophet or preacher says, "Sure, but look at the blood moons and the sun eclipses and the once-in-a-lifetime alignment of Halley's comet, Venus, and the International Space Station." These days, it seems that if you want to know the times, you must be an astronomer, a meteorologist, or an astronaut.

The truth is that you don't need a PhD after your name to understand God's times. You simply need a desire to learn and the discipline to study His Word. The Holy Spirit will take care of the rest.

WE ARE TO USE TIME WISELY WHILE TIME IS STILL AROUND TO BE USED

Although we cannot know the exact day of Jesus' return, we do know that it is near. Paul wrote,

> Concerning the times and the seasons, brethren, you have no need that I should write to you. For you yourselves

know perfectly that the day of the Lord so comes as a thief in the night. For when they say, "Peace and safety!" then sudden destruction comes upon them, as labor pains upon a pregnant woman. And they shall not escape (1 Thessalonians 5:1-3).

The foreshadowing of the end surrounds us. The slippery slope that the world has been sliding down continues to get steeper. The time that God has appointed to wrap up the church's time on this earth and begin Israel's discipline could come at any moment. Knowing this, how do we then live?

In his first letter, Peter gave a detailed response to this question:

The end of all things is at hand; therefore be serious and watchful in your prayers. And above all things have fervent love for one another, for "love will cover a multitude of sins." Be hospitable to one another without grumbling. As each one has received a gift, minister it to one another, as good stewards of the manifold grace of God. If anyone speaks, let him speak as the oracles of God. If anyone ministers, let him do it as with the ability which God supplies, that in all things God may be glorified through Jesus Christ, to whom belong the glory and the dominion forever and ever. Amen (1 Peter 4:7-11).

Peter begins by affirming that the end is near. The concept of time is about to dissolve. It started, and it is going to end (Revelation 22:1-5). Before that was eternity. And after that is eternity. Think about that—for the first time in history, mankind will be transferred into the eternal realm. Time will no longer affect us. Our glorified bodies won't need to worry about wrinkles and baggy eyes and male-pattern baldness. How can time take a toll on us if there is no time? I don't know about you, but just thinking about living outside of time short-circuits my brain. It is the only context where the phrase "You have no future" is actually a positive statement. It feels illogical and sounds irrational, but that is simply because time is all we know. For now, having "no future" is still in the future.

While we still quite literally have time, Peter tells us to be about God's business. We are called to be serious and watchful, not frivolous and self-focused. Ours should be sacrificial lives of love, sharing with others the physical and spiritual blessings given to us by the Holy Spirit. Peter understood this better than most. He heard from Jesus' own mouth our great commission to spread the gospel to this world. He knew that this was the very reason the Lord was delaying His return, and that is the reason He continues to delay it today. "Beloved, do not forget this one thing, that with the Lord one day is as a thousand years, and a thousand years as one day. The Lord is not slack concerning His promise, as some count slackness, but is longsuffering toward us, not willing that any should perish but that all should come to repentance" (2 Peter 3:8-9).

Jesus said, "Surely I am coming quickly" (Revelation 22:20). But His coming will not happen until the time the Lord has already chosen for His long-suffering to come to an end. We are in that window of opportunity. We must use it to the full. So while one part of our hearts answers Jesus' promise of a quick return, saying, "Amen, Even so, come, Lord Jesus!" (Revelation 22:20), the other part says, "Give me just a little more time, Father, so I can lead just one more soul to repentance."

PART 3:

TWO PATHS IN REVELATION

CHAPTER 7

THE BEGINNING OF THE END

Welcome to the Apocalypse

All creation is moving minute by minute, day by day, to a time when time is no more. But not all paths to that final destination are the same. Israel has one path, the church has another, and those who are not a part of either Israel or the church have a third. In these next chapters, we will focus on God's plans for Israel and the church. While these two tracks are separate right now, there is coming a time when they will converge for a while before finally merging into one. As our roadmap for these two routes, we will use the book of Revelation.

I will be very honest with you. In the past it wasn't easy for me to teach on this great apocalyptic book. I struggled with it for a long time as a young believer, and I even tended to avoid it as I grew in my faith. I believe that this is the case for many Christians. The book is scary and, at times, just weird. Sometimes it almost feels as if one is reading a science fiction novel or a work of fantasy complete with kings and dragons and great beasts. Revelation can be spooky and frightening and incredibly confusing. So many people take the same attitude I had: "I can live my life just fine without learning and studying the book of Revelation. I'd rather leave it alone."

Now that I've taken time to learn this book, that attitude of avoidance breaks my heart. By ignoring Revelation, the believer misses so much. This is the only one of the sixty-six books of the Bible that God specifically promises a blessing to all who read and obey its content. "Blessed is he who reads and those who hear the words of this prophecy, and keep those things which are written in it; for the time is near" (Revelation 1:3).

This formula of "learning + obeying = blessing" is a common theme in Scripture. When Ezra described his journey to Jerusalem, he wrote,

> On the first day of the first month he began his journey from Babylon, and on the first day of the fifth month he came to Jerusalem, according to the good hand of his God upon him. For Ezra had prepared his heart to seek the Law of the LORD, and to do it, and to teach statutes and ordinances in Israel (Ezra 7:9-10).

The good hand of God was on this faithful leader and scribe. Why? The word "For" answers the question. God blessed Ezra because he sought God's law, obeyed it, and taught it to others. If you are seeking the blessing of the God of all creation, you'll find it in the pages of Scripture and in your commitment to follow what you read. When it comes to reading Revelation, the apostle John tells us this is especially true.

"But, Amir, is Revelation really applicable to our lives? Sure it's interesting and all, but I want to learn how I should live today!" This belief that there are no real-life applications in Revelation is a common misunderstanding of this amazing book. Go back to John's words we read earlier. He said, "Blessed is he who reads and those who hear the words of the prophecy, *and keep those things which are written in it.*" If there is nothing applicable—no "now do this" or "that is how you should now live"—then how are we going to "keep those things"? There are pastors and teachers who sidestep this book because of its supposed lack of relevance to the Christian's daily life. This is a tragedy. Such avoidance keeps the members of their churches from the full counsel of God, and it holds out of the reach of their people the specific blessings that the Lord has connected to the book of Revelation.

First on the list of those who want you to ignore this book is Satan himself. Why? Because nobody wants others to read about their ultimate defeat. Revelation describes the end of all things, including the devil and his minions. In fact, I believe with all my heart that the only one who gains from believers not studying any specific part of God's Word is Satan. Without this book, he can put forth the illusion that he still has great power. This false narrative of the devil's power postulates that there is a great battle between good and evil in this world and that the ultimate outcome is up for grabs.

If you are looking for truth about the world's past, present, and future, the only place to find it is in God's Word.

The popularity of this false plotline is due more to the influence of movies, television, and novels than it is by Scripture. This should come as no surprise. Think about how much more time the average Christian spends each day involved in some sort of entertainment compared to the few minutes they put into studying the Bible. If you are looking for truth about the world's past, present, and future, the only place to find it is in God's Word. It is the only record we have that provides a full and accurate picture of not only the heart of God, but of His plans.

THE BOOK OF REVELATION 101

Let's move now to how the book of Revelation came about. First, we need to establish the time of its writing. The reason this is so important is that there are those who say that because of when the book was written, it is irrelevant to us today. Why? They claim that all the events talked about by John have already taken place. They say that while it spoke to the devastating near future of the original readers, it's just a somewhat-hard-to-follow historical narrative for us today.

Those who hold to this viewpoint are called *preterists*, which comes from the Latin word *praeter*, meaning "past." They say that what John describes in Revelation *was* fulfilled in the *past*, rather than *will* be fulfilled in the *future*. Usually going hand in hand with preterism is the belief that God's connection with Israel ended in AD 70 when Jerusalem was sacked by the Romans and the Temple was destroyed. From that point on, the "Plan B" church filled the place in God's salvation strategy that was once held by His failed "Plan A" people—the Jews. As we've seen, this is the foundational premise of Replacement Theology—the belief that God has permanently rejected Israel and given all of the nation's promises to the church.

Preterism affects how one must date the book of Revelation. For the events described to be referring to the sacking of Jerusalem in AD 70, the book had to have been written in the late AD 60s. Preterists say all the horrors described in Revelation were figuratively fulfilled by the severe persecution of Christians under Emperor Nero's bloody reign, before the great destructive culmination when Emperor Vespasian ordered the city to be levelled in AD 70. However, it takes some manipulation and a lot of allegorizing of content to make that date fit because so much of what is described simply has no real-world historical correlation.

For example, the year AD 70 did not have the lake of fire. It did not mark the beginning of the millennial kingdom. There was no great leader who performed unbelievable events like resurrecting himself from the dead. Either you have to look at Revelation and say that those passages don't actually mean what they appear to mean, or you have to admit that they are yet to come. The preterist authorship date of the late AD 60s is wholly incompatible with a literal interpretation of Scripture. Therefore, the date of its authorship must be after Jerusalem's destruction.

Another reason to hold to a later authorship—AD 95–96—is the location where the book was written. John wrote, "I, John, your brother and partner in the tribulation and the kingdom and the patient endurance that are in Jesus, was on the island called Patmos on account of the word of God and the testimony of Jesus" (Revelation 1:9 ESV).

The second-century church father Irenaeus asserts that John's exile at Patmos took place during the latter part of the reign of the Emperor Domitian (AD 81–96). Eusebius, writing in the early fourth century, affirmed Irenaeus's date.

This later date not only removes the need for allegorizing the text, but it also fits history better. The book was written more than two decades after the destruction of Jerusalem and the Temple. Thus, there is no mention in the book of sacrificial ceremonies going on in the city. In fact, there is no mention of any events prior to AD 70, nor any specific discourse about the Jewish revolt or the coming demolition of the Temple. If pre-AD 70 Jerusalem was truly the *Sitz im Leben* of authorship, it is reasonable to think that there would have been some precise or detailed information about God's holy city in that time. But there is nothing specific to first-century Jerusalem. In actuality, the judgments of Revelation are global in scope. We see God bringing the hammer down upon the whole world, not just one city.

Besides the date, there is one other foundational matter that biblical "scholars" tend to attack—the book's authorship. Numerous non-Johannine theories put forth various potential writers. One popular theory says that the writer of the book could very well have been an elder from the church of Ephesus who found himself exiled to the island of Patmos. This man wrote his own vision—then in order to garner credibility, he signed John's name to it. But one only needs to look at the rest of John's writings to see that this book fits him to a *t*.

John was very much into signs, and the number seven was important to him. Looking at his Gospel, we see it is filled with mentions of miraculous signs. He tells of Jesus changing water into wine (John 2:1-11), healing the official's son (4:46-54), healing the paralyzed man at the pool of Bethesda (5:1-15), feeding the 5,000 (6:5-14), walking on water (6:16-24), healing the man born blind (9:1-7), and raising Lazarus from the dead (11:1-45). John included these seven signs in his Gospel to prove that Jesus is indeed the promised Messiah. He is not just a man; He is Immanuel—God with us. In Revelation, we also find this emphasis on signs and miracles, and the number seven is extant throughout—seven seals, seven trumpets, seven bowls. Even the writing style and the use of layman's Greek, which are hallmarks of John's writing, are evident in Revelation.

The later date of writing, along with John as the author, best fits the style and content of the book. Why is there so much effort these days to make the book seem as if it is either irrelevant or written by an imposter? It goes back to the promise of blessing from Revelation 1:3. The devil is trying to rob you of the favor of God that comes from reading, understanding, and doing what is contained in this book. He wants to keep you from experiencing the fullness of the Lord's revelatory Word. Consider how special this book is! John wrote, "The Revelation of Jesus Christ, which God gave Him to show His servants—things which must shortly take place. And He sent and signified it by His angel to His servant John, who bore witness to the word of God, and to the testimony of Jesus Christ, to all things that he saw" (Revelation 1:1-2). God had a message so important that He chose His Son to deliver it in person. And the content to be passed on was so incredible, so mind-blowing that it wasn't enough just to *tell* John—He had to *show* these things to this disciple so beloved by the Savior. The apostle didn't just hear about the things to come, he saw them with his own eyes. Again, it's no wonder why the enemy is trying so hard to keep believers from reading this book.

God is not just guessing about the future. He already knows.

A PREVIEW OF WHAT IS TO COME

The more I study the book of Revelation, the more I love it. It's like the movie *Back to the Future*. When we read it, we go back in time to a moment when God Himself revealed to us the future He has established for this world. What we read is not what might happen or could happen. It is what absolutely 100 percent *will* happen. God is not just guessing about the future. He already knows. He's watched the film; He's streamed the video. In fact, He wrote the script and directed the entire movie.

In Revelation, God is showing us the trailer of what is to come—the movie preview. We don't get to see all the details, but we learn enough to know the plotline. It's going to be an action movie with a lot of violence. But it is also a romance, complete with a wedding and a huge banquet. But there is one problem with this preview—the Director gives away the ending! But while in the film world that's a box-office no-no, in this case, knowing how it all ends should make us even more excited to watch the plot unfold.

Why does God give us the spoiler that reveals the end of all things? It's not simply to quench our curiosity or so that we can show others that we know more than they do. It is so we are aware of the destinies of both believers and unbelievers. It is to encourage those of us who follow Christ in a world that is so evil. Do you feel beaten down by the rampant immorality and anti-God attitude of our culture? Take heart—God has a plan that He will implement in His time for our benefit. And that time is near!

Now, why do we think that the events described in Revelation are near when John wrote it 2,000 years ago? How can we say that today might be the day of Christ's return? If this hasn't happened by now, can we still believe that it is ever going to happen? At some point, doesn't a rational thinker have to step back and say, "Well, obviously we got that interpretation wrong"?

The answer to these questions goes back to our understanding of time. For us, it seems like it has been forever since John wrote Revelation. But remember: God experiences time differently. He is outside of time. He is not late. Instead, as we saw earlier in 2 Peter 3:8-9, He is long-suffering. He is giving the people of the world more time to repent. One of the benefits of the COVID pandemic is that it has spurred many people to reevaluate their lives—to look at what is important to them and examine how they use their time. People have slowed down enough that they are asking themselves about where they stand with God. "What will happen if I get this virus? What will happen if I die alone in a hospital room? Is that all there is? Am I ready for when this life ends?"

While we should never celebrate a pandemic, we can be thankful for how God has used it. Judgment time is near. "As it is appointed for men to die once, but after this the judgment" (Hebrews 9:27). We live, we die, then judgment. Once judgment comes, that's it. There are no second chances. What peace comes from knowing that the Lord is a righteous judge! However one might be punished or rewarded, we can be assured that it will completely fair and will be based on the grace, mercy, and justice of the perfect, sovereign God.

Soon the Restrainer will be removed and God's wrath will be poured out upon this ungodly world. It's time to tell the full story and keep nothing from anyone. This is the essence of the book of Revelation. We must remember that much of what we read is them versus us. In other words, it is not about us as believers; rather, it is about them— the unbelievers. The tribulation is not about us as the church, but them—Israel. Church-age Christians will not remain on this earth to experience the judgments. But it is still for us to know what will take place. Otherwise, the information would not have been given to John to write. Revelation is for believers to read and understand because we are the ones God intends to bless through the book. It was also given by God because He wants us to understand that He is aware of what is going on around the world. He knows how bad things are and that they will continue to get worse. And He *will* do something about that.

We need to hold on to these truths. Jesus is risen, as promised. He will return to take us, as promised. He will reign over the world, as promised. And He will judge all peoples, as promised.

THE MESSENGER AND THE MESSAGE

An old man sits on a rock with his eyes closed. His long beard gently pulls to the left as it rides the morning breeze. He is so still that it is hard to tell whether he is sleeping or praying. The answer becomes evident when his brows furl and his lips move almost imperceptibly as he whispers. After a few seconds, he again becomes still, and the only sounds are the water gently lapping on the shore around him and the calls of the gulls overhead looking for tiny crabs or urchins or any leftover scraps from the man's meager breakfast of bread and a little dried fish.

Looking at his thin, rickety body alone on this rocky beach, it is hard to imagine the storied life he has led. Raised as a fisherman by his father, Zebedee, he and his older brother, James, were destined to take over their father's boats and business. Then one day a man came along who changed his life's direction forever. This wise and loving miracle-worker called for James and John—along with business partners Simon and Andrew—to follow Him. And to their own astonishment and that of everyone they knew, these rugged men found themselves leaving their boats to become His acolytes.

Many who knew James and John had to be shaking their heads. "Really? These guys? They're the new followers of this holy man?" The two brothers were known for their tempers, causing their new teacher, Jesus, to give them the nickname *Boanerges*—the sons of thunder. One day after Jesus and His disciples had been snubbed by a town full of Samaritans, it was the Thunder Bros. who ran to Jesus and said, "Lord, do You want us to command fire to come down from heaven and consume them, just as Elijah did?" (Luke 9:54). Jesus calmed them down, reminding them that He had come to save people, not to turn them into crispy critters.

Along with Simon, whom Jesus had rechristened Peter, these sons of Zebedee made up the Savior's inner circle. As a result, they were given access to teachings and witnessed events that the other nine disciples were not privy to, such as the raising of Jairus's daughter and Jesus' transfiguration, during which they came face to face with Moses and Elijah.

John went on to develop a deep love for his teacher, one which often caused later artistic depicters to paint him as soft and effeminate. "At the last supper, John laid against Jesus' breast, which doesn't sound too manly to me," they might have supposed. But that kind of physical contact is simply an expression of friendship in Middle Eastern culture. Even today, it is not unusual to find two old men laughing and telling stories as they walk hand in hand down the street. No, John and his brother James were two sea-salted, callous-handed fishermen ready to rumble with anyone who may have looked at them sideways.

John was at the cross when Jesus was crucified, and he was the first to put two and two together about the rolled-away stone and the resurrection, telling the readers of his Gospel that when he entered the empty tomb, "he saw and believed" (John 20:8). He saw Christ ascend into heaven, and was one of the transformed and Holy Spirit-empowered preachers who poured out into the crowds on the Day of Pentecost. John was involved in the founding of the first church in Jerusalem and endured tremendous grief when his brother James was killed by King Herod and became the first disciple to suffer martyrdom. At some point, John traveled to the Roman city of Ephesus, quite possibly taking with him Jesus' mother, Mary, whose care had been entrusted to him by Jesus Himself while the Savior was hanging on the cross. In Ephesus, during the Christian persecution under Emperor Domitian, John was arrested and exiled to the tiny Mediterranean island of Patmos. This is where this passionate, transformed lover of people and former confidante of Christ was living when he was surprised by a voice calling to him from behind.

Because of the unusual nature of the message found in the book of Revelation, it is easy to miss the truth that this was written by a real person to other real people. This is unfortunate. Once authorship becomes generic and the audience becomes generic, the message will become generic. Rather than it being a letter of hope and comfort from a true apostle and close compatriot of Christ to seven churches that were enduring persecution under a harsh emperor, it devolves into some hard-to-understand message written by some guy to some people for some reason or another. The more that specificity is lost, the easier it is to allegorize the content and generalize the meaning.

Instead, right off the bat, John makes it clear to the readers both who is writing this book and to whom he is writing it: "John, to the seven church which are in Asia" (Revelation 1:4). While John fully expects this to be read throughout the church for ages to come, he has a specific audience and a special message of hope to give to them:

> Grace to you and peace from Him who is and who was and
> who is to come, and from the seven Spirits who are before
> His throne, and from Jesus Christ, the faithful witness, the
> firstborn from the dead, and the ruler over the kings of
> the earth…Behold, He is coming with clouds, and every
> eye will see Him, even they who pierced Him. And all the
> tribes of the earth will mourn because of Him. Even so,
> Amen (Revelation 1:4-5,7).

The eternal God sees you and sends His blessing of grace and peace, as
does Jesus Christ our Savior, who is coming again to rescue us from
this world.

Imagine the comfort; imagine the encouragement. The one who
is the Alpha and the Omega—the *Aleph* and the *Tav*—the Almighty
Creator knows about you in Ephesus and Smyrna, in Pergamum and
Thyatira, in Sardis, Philadelphia, and even in wishy-washy Laodicea.
This letter is sent out to you to let you have a glimpse into My plans so
that you know that evil does not win out. The Roman Empire will not
last forever. Satan does not have the upper hand. God will win. Judgment will come against the world and against the Jews. But reward will
also come—for the church and for the Jews. So read these words, live
them out, and you will be blessed by God, because these words lead to
the grace and peace that come from resting in the loving and just sovereignty of the Almighty.

Picture John sitting on a rock on the shore of Patmos. Maybe it was
early in the morning and he was enjoying a cool breeze blowing off
the water. Maybe it was the end of the day and all the aches and pains
of an old fisherman were making him wonder if he had the energy to
cook up the little that he had caught for his evening meal. As he rested,
he suddenly heard a booming voice call from behind, "I am the Alpha
and the Omega…Write what you see in a book and send it to the seven
churches, to Ephesus and to Smyrna and to Pergamum and to Thyatira and to Sardis and to Philadelphia and to Laodicea" (Revelation
1:11 ESV). I wonder if John even heard anything after that first sentence,
that introduction. He knew that title. There was only one voice to
whom those appellations belonged.

Fearful, excited, filled with anticipation, John slowly turned around. There stood his Lord, his teacher, his friend—Jesus. But this did not look like the same Jesus whom he last saw floating up into heaven. While the human side of the Savior would likely have still made Him quite recognizable, this was Jesus Christ in full-on God mode. Surrounded by seven golden lampstands stood "One like the Son of Man, clothed with a garment down to the feet and girded about the chest with a golden band. His head and hair were white like wool, as white as snow, and His eyes like a flame of fire; His feet were like fine brass, as if refined in a furnace, and His voice as the sound of many waters; He had in His right hand seven stars, out of His mouth went a sharp two-edged sword, and His countenance was like the sun shining in its strength" (Revelation 1:13-16). The sight was so magnificent that John took one look and all his old, wiry muscles turned to jelly. He dropped to the ground.

Then John felt a touch. Imagine that moment. It had been sixty years since he had felt a touch from that hand. It was a touch of love, of peace, of grace and blessing and strength sufficient to fortify his old bones to endure the journey that lay ahead. Jesus spoke again, this time softer: "Do not be afraid; I am the First and the Last. I am He who lives, and was dead, and behold, I am alive forevermore. Amen. And I have the keys of Hades and of Death" (Revelation 1:17-18). John likely would have sat up as Jesus explained why He had come. "I have a job for you. I want you to write down what you're about to see." Maybe John looked around for the seven golden lampstands and the seven stars Jesus had been holding, which were now missing, so the Lord explained, "The mystery of the seven stars which you saw in My right hand, and the seven golden lampstands: The seven stars are the angels of the seven churches, and the seven lampstands which you saw are the seven churches" (Revelation 1:20).

How encouraging would it have been to the churches reading the letter to know that not only did they have their own lampstand in the presence of Jesus, but their own angel as well? How do you feel knowing that your congregation at the Third Baptist Church of West Akron or wherever you fellowship has an angel of its own? As the American progressive movement continues to chip away at religious freedom and a church's First Amendment rights, how fortifying is it to know that your church's lampstand is in the presence of the Almighty?

Once Jesus got John calmed down, the disciple found his writing kit. Settling in a place where John could write—maybe down by the water or at a table in his home or shelter—Jesus began dictating as John wrote down the words.

CHAPTER 8

THE CHURCH
IN REVELATION

The Groom Speaks to His Betrothed

Jesus dictated and John wrote, and out of this great collaborative duo came seven brief but amazing letters. What did this process look like? It's hard to know because John suspended his narration for a time. Rather than giving us a glimpse into the writing process, he simply delivered us the result—missives from God directed toward seven key churches in an area that is currently part of southern Turkey. Did Jesus deliver these words in the same trumpet-blast voice that contained the "sound of many waters" (Revelation 1:15)? Did He continue to shine with the strength of the sun, making Him almost impossible to gaze at for any length of time? One might think so, if it wasn't for that hand that touched John.

As we saw last chapter, when John's old legs gave out, Jesus laid His right hand on him. What started out as a royal introduction of divine proportions suddenly became intimate. Creator-announcing-to-creation became Master-comforting-servant, Rabbi-reassuring-student, Friend-touching-friend. The grand symbolic displays had departed. When John looked up, the golden lampstands representing the seven churches were gone. The seven angelic stars had vacated the Lord's right hand to make room for His disciple's shoulder. All that was left were John and his Savior. We can only speculate as to the scene, but I picture a much-more-stable John sitting down with his writing kit, a piece of parchment prepared before him, and a stylus ready in his hand. Meanwhile, a less-shiny, more-indoor-voiced Jesus began to slowly pace. After a moment, John's hand started moving as Jesus spoke: "To the angel of the church of Ephesus write…" (Revelation 2:1).

EPHESUS—THE LOST LOVE

How John's ears must have perked up when Jesus started with his home church. What was the Lord going to tell his congregation? Was He going to give them a "Well done" for all their good work, or was He going to chastise them? John had been in that church a long time. He had seen it in its prime, and he knew the state it was currently in. It was likely that he expected that Jesus would give the Ephesian church a little of both—a thumbs up and a thumbs down. If that was what he was anticipating, then he would have been right.

Ephesus was one of the great cities of its time, and because it was John's home, we'll spend a little more time with it. It was known as the Mother City of Asia, although that may not be quite as grandiose as it seems. At that time, Asia did not encompass an entire continent as it does today. Back then, it was simply one of the more important of the Roman provinces. The third-largest city in the empire, Ephesus was home to a quarter of a million people.

This city was politically important because it was the capital of the senatorial province of Asia. There were two types of provinces in the empire—senatorial and imperial. Those that were senatorial were Roman through and through. There was no concern over revolts or uprisings. The people in these provinces loved Rome, and Rome loved them. The imperial provinces, however, were a little more sketchy. These people were part of the empire because Rome said so. They were usually on the outskirts of the empire's boundaries and were prone to rebellion. In which of these two provincial categories would you expect to find Judea? If you said imperial, then Simon the Zealot would be very proud of you.

Besides being the capital city of an important province, Ephesus was also religiously important. It was home to the great temple of Artemis (also known as Diana). One of the Seven Wonders of the Ancient World, this magnificent structure was the largest building known in antiquity. Four times as large as the Parthenon of Athens, its columns rose sixty feet into the air. People would come from all over the empire to worship at this temple. In the same way that Salt Lake City, Utah, is the center of Mormonism, Ephesus was the center of Artemis worship. Thus, there existed in the city a vibrant idol industry, with figurines of Diana being sold to locals and the many visitors.

This idol trade is what led to the famous riot of Ephesus that Luke reported in the book of Acts. When Demetrius the silversmith saw Christianity cutting into his profits, he gathered his fellow tradesmen. Soon their rally turned into a protest as they began marching and chanting "Great is Artemis of the Ephesians!" (Acts 19:24 esv). As more people joined, the protest became a riot. Luke is unclear whether there was any breaking of windows, looting of electronics, spray-painting of vulgarities, or defunding of the police, but soon the mob found themselves in the local amphitheater, where they chanted "Great is Artemis of the Ephesians!" for about two hours.

Eventually, the city clerk quieted the people down, saying, "Men of Ephesus, who is there who does not know that the city of the Ephesians is temple keeper of the great Artemis, and of the sacred stone that fell from the sky? Seeing then that these things cannot be denied, you ought to be quiet and do nothing rash" (Acts 19:35-36 esv). While we may disagree with the clerk as to what is and is not undeniable, he did manage to calm everyone and send them home.

A third way that Ephesus was important was commercially. It was perfectly situated for trade. The eastbound road to Colossae and Laodicea, the northbound road to Smyrna, and the northeastbound road to Sardis and Galatia all converged at this seaport city. Thus, it became the largest trading center in Asia Minor. All that shipping and business meant that Ephesus was a nasty city. After the sailors brought their boats into port, they wanted a little time off and a bit of companionship that was far more pretty and far less male than what they had been cooped up with for the previous weeks. Between the sexualized worship of Artemis and the hedonism of the port districts, those in the Ephesian church faced a strong and pervasive temptation to indulge in immorality.

But breaking through this thick blanket of sin was a brilliant ray of light. The gospel came to Ephesus, and, like moths to a flame, people flew to it. In the midst of all the emptiness and nihilism of the debauchery, hope was born into the hearts of many—and with that hope came joy and love. The church at Ephesus was born. Because of the radical change required from the lifestyle of the culture, becoming a new servant of Christ took discipline and commitment. The onslaught of persecution was met with resolve. Mockery from outside the church was met with a strengthening unity within the church. The birth of the Ephesian church would have been a period during which members were held together by a fierce love for one another and, even more so, for their Savior.

Then the years passed and the church became stronger, more established. Threats from silversmiths and others were still present, but the possibility of attack was not as great as in the early years. The first generation of church planters had passed, and the church was now likely run by their grown children or even grandchildren. These succeeding generations knew the gospel and the Word of God, and consequently were able to maintain a purity of doctrine:

> I know your works, your labor, your patience, and that you
> cannot bear those who are evil. And you have tested those
> who say they are apostles and are not, and have found them
> liars; and you have persevered and have patience, and have
> labored for My name's sake and have not become weary
> (Revelation 2:2-3).

When heresies, like those of the Nicolaitans (which we will examine with the church of Pergamum) popped up, the Ephesians were sure to put them back down.

Yet despite all these positives, there was a negative. It was glaring, prevalent, and very dangerous. Jesus told the church, "Nevertheless I have this against you, that you have left your first love. Remember therefore from where you have fallen; repent and do the first works, or else I will come to you quickly and remove your lampstand from its place—unless you repent" (Revelation 2:4-5). How did John feel when he heard these words? Was he floored—shocked at his church being called out? Or, in his heart, was he saying, "Thank You, Lord! I've been trying to relight a fire in them for years"?

This church was in a precarious situation. If the problem had been immorality or bad doctrine, it could have been rooted out and dealt with—like cutting out a tumor. But this was a systemic heart issue. This wasn't a matter of stopping what you're doing wrong, but of changing your priorities and passions. Unfortunately, it is easy for us to let the excitement of salvation and a new relationship with Jesus Christ fade over time. In a marriage, the fiery romance of courting and being a newlywed is typically unsustainable long-term. When the flames begin to subside, a marriage will go one of two directions. One direction leads to distancing and roaming eyes and eventual failure. The second leads to a deeper, more mature love. Like the orange coals of a barbecue pit, this heat is great, enduring, and more productive.

Where are you in your relationship with your Savior? Has your initial excitement been replaced by routine? Has your sacrificial love for God turned into inconvenient obedience? Have you lost your first love?

As He almost always does, the Lord finishes with a word of hope. "To him who overcomes I will give to eat from the tree of life, which is in the midst of the Paradise of God" (Revelation 2:7). Rather than this being a conditional "if…then" statement, it is an encouragement to all those who, through Christ, have overcome the pull of the devil and the world and their own flesh, and have instead offered themselves up to their Lord and Master. They are the ones who will taste the fruit of the tree of life, having secured their place with Christ for eternity. John must have been greatly encouraged as he wrote, for these words likely reminded him that very soon his sojourn on this earth would end, and he and his visiting old Friend would be together forever.

SMYRNA—THE
ATTRACTIVENESS OF SUFFERING

Jesus now begins His clockwise "visits" to the seven churches with a move to the northwest. Smyrna, which means "myrrh," was another important trade city like Ephesus. However, unlike the now-abandoned larger city, this one still exists today. Now known as Izmir, it is the third largest metropolis in Turkey with a population of more than four million people.

After greeting the church in Smyrna, the Lord says through John's writing,

> I know your works, tribulation, and poverty (but you are rich); and I know the blasphemy of those who say they are Jews and are not, but are a synagogue of Satan. Do not fear any of those things which you are about to suffer. Indeed, the devil is about to throw some of you into prison, that you may be tested, and you will have tribulation ten days. Be faithful until death, and I will give you the crown of life (Revelation 2:9-10).

Notice the words Jesus uses—suffer, prison, tested, tribulation, death. Not great words of encouragement.

For the church members, the two most hopeful words had to be the ones that begin verse 9: "I know." The Christians in Smyrna, despite working hard at serving the Lord, were suffering. There are two types of persecution that were happening in those days and that still affect many thousands of Christians around the world today. One is direct persecution—violence, imprisonment, death. The second is ostracization. This can be even more devastating because it affects the well-being of the entire family. In cultures with one predominant non-Christian religion, it is not unusual for Christian conversion to result in a breaking of ties by family members, loss of employment and employability, and even a barring from any commercial transactions. This leaves believers all alone with no money, no way to make money, and no place to spend the money even if they had it.

The Christians in Smyrna seem to have been experiencing both kinds of persecution, leading to "tribulation and poverty." But rather than saying, "I'm going to end your suffering," Jesus' message is, "I know that you're suffering, and it's about to get worse." He says, "Indeed, the devil is about to throw some of you into prison, that you may be tested, and you will have tribulation ten days" (Revelation 2:10). Some people may ask, "What's the use of following an all-powerful God if all He will do when the times get tough is sit back and say, 'Wow, kinda stinks to be you' "? That's a fair question.

John knew the power of those words "I know." He had written them numerous times in his Gospel. Those words speak of relationship and protection: "I am the good shepherd; and I know My sheep, and am known by My own" (John 10:14). They speak of intention and identity: "I know whom I have chosen" (John 13:18). The church in Smyrna was "known" by Jesus and was therefore directly under His loving oversight. Therefore, the people could be assured that in spite of the pain of their suffering, what they faced was actually a good thing. Though they were poor when it came to material goods, they were rich in the spiritual realm. Though they struggled to feed their families, their heavenly bank accounts had extremely high balances.

Their Good Shepherd reminded His sheep of this, saying, "Be faithful until death, and I will give you the crown of life. He who has an ear, let him hear what the Spirit says to the churches. He who overcomes shall not be hurt by the second death" (Revelation 2:10-11). Persecution would come for the church of Smyrna from both the Jews and the Gentiles. We, too, may suffer from persecution or the trials of life. However, any suffering we experience now will not compare with the misery of those who will endure the fires of hell—the second death. We are not destined for that. Instead, to us belongs the crown of life.

PERGAMUM—DEFENDING THE TRUTH IN A CULTURE OF LIES

Truth matters. You can gather a group of people, sing songs, talk about spiritual things, love each other, meet regularly, and do good deeds for the needy—those are all fine ways to spend your time. But if you are not centered on the Word of God, then don't call yourself a church—you're not. You're a social club. You're no different than the Elks Club or the Shriners or the Loyal Order of Water Buffaloes, except that your meetings are held in a big building with a cross on it. Sadly, this lack of grounding in the Bible describes many churches today, particularly those in the mainline denominations.

Moving north another forty miles through Asia Minor, Jesus' focus now settles on the church in Pergamum. This was another large city, known for its production of parchment. It was a place of learning that drew people in from across the Roman Empire. Not only did the city produce parchment, but it had a vast library to store the many works written on its parchment, and a large university created for scholars to study those same works. Yet even though it was a city of the mind, it was also a city of the spirit. But the spiritual side of Pergamum tended toward the very dark.

Jesus says, "I know your works, and where you dwell, where Satan's throne is. And you hold fast to My name, and did not deny My faith even in the days in which Antipas was My faithful martyr, who was killed among you, where Satan dwells" (Revelation 2:13). In Pergamum sat both an altar for Zeus and an altar for Lucifer—the latter known as the seat of Satan. You would think that in a city such as this the Christians would face a lot of persecution. But that wasn't the case. Yes, during a time of strife, a man named Antipas was martyred there allegedly by being roasted alive in a bull-shaped bronze altar. Yet Satan discovered that such persecution ended up strengthening the church. So he changed tactics. Rather than attacking the church from the outside as he did in Smyrna, he began corrupting it from the inside.

The leaders of the church began to allow the teaching of false doctrine:

> I have a few things against you, because you have there those who hold the doctrine of Balaam, who taught Balak to put a stumbling block before the children of Israel, to eat things sacrificed to idols, and to commit sexual immorality. Thus you also have those who hold the doctrine of the Nicolaitans, which thing I hate (Revelation 2:14-15).

There has been much speculation over the identity and beliefs of the Nicolaitans. Unfortunately, there is no strong evidence we can examine that clearly identifies them. This passage gives us at least some information, linking them to those who followed the "doctrine of Balaam."

We've looked at Balaam's story already—his being hired by King Balak to curse the Israelites and his inability to carry out that task due to God's intervention. However, Balaam's story didn't end with that incident. Rather than returning home, the prophet appears to have stuck around. Instead of tearing at Israel from the outside, he began attacking from the inside by convincing many of the Israelite men to allow their eHarmony and Tinder accounts to include the idol-following Moabite and Midianite women. This was directly contrary to the command of God, yet the Israelite men ate it up—swiping right on their app for every available foreign woman they could find.

Balaam's plan worked perfectly. People ignored the Word of God, and sin's cancer ate away on the inside. Men's hearts were turned from God, and they began engaging in the idol worship of the Baal of Peor. Eventually God called upon Moses to purify the camp of those caught up in this heretical rebellion, which he did with bloody efficiency. Not long after, the Lord turned His sights outward and called for vengeance upon those who had led the Israelites into sin. Balaam, who was still around and probably enjoying the fruits of his labors, was caught up in this purge, and we read that "Balaam the son of Beor they also killed with the sword" (Numbers 31:8).

When Jesus introduces Himself to the church in Pergamum, He says, "These things says He who has the sharp two-edged sword" (Revelation 2:12). Later, after He identifies their heresies, He warns, "Repent, or else I will come to you quickly and will fight against them with the sword of My mouth" (Revelation 2:16). Why the emphasis on a sword? When sin and heresy flooded into the Israelite camp, the Lord rooted them out with a sword. What would it take to root out the sin and heresy from the church in Pergamum? Again, a sword.

What is this sword Jesus speaks of? When Paul tells the Ephesians to put on the full armor of God, he tells them to take up the sword of the Spirit, "which is the word of God" (Ephesians 6:17). The writer of Hebrews compared the Bible with a sword when he wrote, "The word of God is living and powerful, and sharper than any two-edged sword, piercing even to the division of soul and spirit, and of joints and marrow, and is a discerner of the thoughts and intents of the heart" (Hebrews 4:12). Why would Jesus come with a sword? Because it is the sword of the Word of God that identifies and cuts out any heresy and rebellion that the enemy may use to infiltrate a church.

What is it that sets Christians apart from the rest of the world? It is our absolute commitment to the Word of God.

This would have resonated with John as he wrote. He would have remembered the prayer in the upper room so many years ago—a prayer he later recorded verbatim in his Gospel. Jesus implored the Father, "Sanctify them by Your truth. Your word is truth" (John 17:17). To be sanctified, or made holy, is to be set apart. What is it that sets Christians apart from the rest of the world? It is our absolute commitment to the Word of God. We have the truth, and that truth sets us free from the lies of our culture. Our churches must be 100 percent loyal to the full Word of God with no compromise. This will ensure that the enemy cannot corrupt our churches or ourselves from the inside. Daily time studying the truth found in God's Word is the best weapon for keeping the devil at bay.

THYATIRA—FINDING A MORAL COMPASS

Jesus' tour of Asia Minor now rounds the top of the clockwise route and begins a semi-straight southeasterly line that will take us to the next four churches. His first stop is the good news/bad news congregation in

Thyatira. Jesus' words start well: "To the angel of the church in Thyatira write, 'These things says the Son of God, who has eyes like a flame of fire, and His feet like fine brass: "I know your works, love, service, faith, and your patience; and as for your works, the last are more than the first"'" (Revelation 2:18-19). The Lord gives them a strong commendation for their commitment to Him. However, those "eyes like a flame of fire" and "feet like fine brass" do sound a little ominous.

Based in the important city of Ephesus and being the last surviving disciple, John likely had his finger on the pulse of all the churches in Asia Minor, as well as many beyond. So it was probably no surprise when the name we are about to read was dropped. It would not even be surprising to find out that John himself may have either sent letters or traveled himself to the small city of Thyatira to confront the church and the woman that Jesus was about to "out" as a false prophetess and an adulteress. Jesus tells the church that if they don't deal with their one bad apple, their whole barrel is in danger of being spoiled.

> Nevertheless I have a few things against you, because you allow that woman Jezebel, who calls herself a prophetess, to teach and seduce My servants to commit sexual immorality and eat things sacrificed to idols. And I gave her time to repent of her sexual immorality, and she did not repent. Indeed I will cast her into a sickbed, and those who commit adultery with her into great tribulation, unless they repent of their deeds. I will kill her children with death, and all the churches shall know that I am He who searches the minds and hearts. And I will give to each one of you according to your works (Revelation 2:20-23).

Purity among God's people is a necessity for a healthy church. Sadly, the trend amongst many churches today is to compromise in areas of sexuality. Biblical mandates against homosexuality and transgenderism are ignored as outdated, ridiculed as intolerant, or swept under the rug because they are just too uncomfortable to talk about. And many of those who continue to stand strong against those sins will turn around menacingly and yell, "Stay out of my bedroom!" when a pastor preaches about heterosexual sex outside of marriage. And if the preacher dares to challenge listeners in the areas of pornography, sensuality, and impure and inappropriate nonmarital sexual activities short of intercourse, he may need a security detail to make it safely to his car.

All sin is rebellion against God and separates us from Him. However, sexual sins are especially heinous because they affect us at a deeper level. Paul wrote about this to the Corinthians, who were dealing with their own church impurity:

> Flee sexual immorality. Every sin that a man does is outside the body, but he who commits sexual immorality sins against his own body. Or do you not know that your body is the temple of the Holy Spirit who is in you, whom you have from God, and you are not your own? For you were bought at a price; therefore glorify God in your body and in your spirit, which are God's (1 Corinthians 6:18-20).

Sexual sin is directed inward. When God designed sex, He made it both a physical and spiritual experience. That is why the two "become one flesh" (Genesis 2:24). In the uniting of two bodies is the uniting of two spirits. One needs only to look at all recorded history up until today to see the countless terrible results that have come from misusing this gift that God bestowed upon the husband and the wife.

A church that accepts sexual sin as okay is not a church that can expect God's blessing. This may be why so many mainline denominations have become bastions of social causes rather than strongholds of truth and lighthouses of the hope that is found in the gospel. But for those Christians and churches who hold tightly to the truth and do not compromise the Word of God, Jesus promises reward. "He who overcomes, and keeps My works until the end, to him I will give power over the nations—'He shall rule them with a rod of iron; they shall be dashed to pieces like the potter's vessels'—as I also have received from My Father; and I will give him the morning star" (Revelation 2:26-28).

If you are in a church that has compromised truth, then it is time to find another church. If you are caught up in these sins yourself, there is time to repent and turn from your ways. Confess your sins to the Lord and ask for His strength to put those actions behind you. If you are living with someone outside of marriage, repent of your wrong choices. God is ready to forgive. Then do what is right. Either get married or separate. It may be difficult, but no one ever said holiness is easy. The Jesus who told the church in Smyrna "I know" knows your situation and will walk the painful and righteous path with you toward the holiness to which our God has called us.

SARDIS—REVIVING A DEAD CHURCH

As we turn the page to Revelation chapter 3—again, continuing in the Lord's message to His future bride, the church—we see Jesus addressing the church in Sardis. John was likely expecting to hear some complimentary words. The Sardinian Christians had the reputation of being passionate servants of God. Word was that the Spirit was moving and so were they—out doing the works of Christ. So, the words Jesus spoke to them were likely surprising for John to hear.

> I know your works, that you have a name that you are alive, but you are dead. Be watchful, and strengthen the things which remain, that are ready to die, for I have not found your works perfect before God. Remember therefore how you have received and heard; hold fast and repent. Therefore if you will not watch, I will come upon you as a thief, and you will not know what hour I will come upon you (Revelation 3:1-3).

The church of Sardis had the reputation of being vibrant, spirit-filled, and obedient to God's Word. But when Jesus looked at the church, He saw a deeper reality. This church was not wicked or immoral like Thyatira. Instead, it was dead and unresponsive to Christ. At some point, the things of God had become rote to them—mindless, automatic. They had stopped being the church and were now simply doing church. There was no more listening to the Spirit of God. There was no seeking His will. They had become religious people who seemed to do a great job of following their rituals. It seems they did it well enough to fool others and probably themselves too. They likely got together each week for their services totally unaware that the Spirit had left the temple.

Every Sunday, congregations around the globe gather. Sadly, for far too many, although their pews are full, their churches are empty. They may have a 2,000-seat sanctuary with a big stage and expensive lighting and multicamera setups that livestream the services to satellite campuses across the city. But what they don't have is what is most important—the Holy Spirit. This lack of Spirit-focus and Spirit-leading is found in a great number of small churches too.

These attendees believe they are doing Christianity right because their pastors and church leaders tell them so. They come to church on Sunday, sing the songs, laugh and cry at the appropriate times during the pastor's entertaining presentation, drop a check in the plate, and head home until next week. Easy peasy, but with no spiritual squeezy. Everybody comes with a smile on their face and everyone leaves with a smile on their face—blessed be the name of the Lord. But is that really what church is supposed to be?

The Lord confronted the failing city of Jerusalem, saying, "These people draw near with their mouths and honor Me with their lips, but have removed their hearts far from Me, and their fear toward Me is taught by the commandment of men" (Isaiah 29:13). These words could have just as easily been directed to those in the church at Sardis, as well as to the church today. But we should not despair. Not all in the church are lost. Jesus said,

> You have a few names even in Sardis who have not defiled their garments; and they shall walk with Me in white, for they are worthy. He who overcomes shall be clothed in white garments, and I will not blot out his name from the Book of Life; but I will confess his name before My Father and before His angels (Revelation 3:4-6).

Just as there were Christians who were still "alive" in Sardis, so are there many churches today that are eagerly seeking to follow the lead of the Holy Spirit. These churches are committed to teaching the Word of God, praying for the will of the Father, preaching the gospel of Jesus Christ, and passionately carrying out the works of the Holy Spirit. Does this describe your church? If not, then you should prayerfully speak to your church's leadership to discover whether you are in a living church or a dead one. If it's dead in the areas that count and the leadership seems content to keep it that way, then it's time to find a new church.

This would also be a good time to evaluate yourself. If Jesus wrote about your church, would you be one of the "worthy" ones who have "not defiled [your] garments"? If you think that you might be one of the dead ones, fear not—life is waiting for you. As Paul wrote, "Awake, you who sleep, arise from the dead, and Christ will give you light" (Ephesians 5:14).

PHILADELPHIA—FIND US FAITHFUL

If Sardis was the bad news, Philadelphia is the good news. As Jesus' journey through the churches continues to the southeast, we pass from death to life. The region of Philadelphia was known for its life—both agricultural and commercial. Located at the entrance to the large central plateau of Asia Minor, vineyards and produce were in abundance. The east-west trade from the western Roman Empire to the kingdoms of Lydia, Mysia, and Phrygia passed through the city, so it was also a hub of commerce and information. That made Philadelphia a perfect location from which to reach wide swaths of the empire with the gospel of Jesus Christ.

To this small but impactful church, the Savior said,

> I know your works. See, I have set before you an open door, and no one can shut it; for you have a little strength, have kept My word, and have not denied My name. Indeed I will make those of the synagogue of Satan, who say they are Jews and are not, but lie—indeed I will make them come and worship before your feet, and to know that I have loved you. Because you have kept My command to persevere, I also will keep you from the hour of trial which shall come upon the whole world, to test those who dwell

on the earth. Behold, I am coming quickly! Hold fast what you have, that no one may take your crown. He who overcomes, I will make him a pillar in the temple of My God, and he shall go out no more. I will write on him the name of My God and the name of the city of My God, the New Jerusalem, which comes down out of heaven from My God. And I will write on him My new name (Revelation 3:8-12).

Picture the scene when the members of this church heard these words read for the first time. Each church had received some good news and bad news, except for Sardis, which was all bad news. The believers at this church likely held their breath when the congregational leader recited the words, "To the angel of the church in Philadelphia write…" (Revelation 3:7). With every successive word, their anxiety would have turned into greater joy. "I know your works…I have set before you an open door…I have loved you…I also will keep you…I am coming quickly!" These are the words that the Lord reserves for the faithful.

Because of Philadelphia's location, the ministry of this church had great reach. Farmers and merchants and traders would all come into the city to do their business. While they were there, the church would reach out to them with the gospel of Christ. Some would respond, receiving the free gift of salvation found in the cross of Jesus. Then they would take their newfound faith with them as they traveled to their next destination or back home. Once there, they would talk about Jesus and His salvation, and more would find Christ. One small church had the potential to reach tens of thousands with the gospel message just by being faithful with what God had given to them—a great location.

Today, technology is the new location. With just a microphone and an internet connection, God allows me to teach biblical truth to hundreds of thousands of people every year right from my home in Israel. Even when the coronavirus shut down church buildings in many countries, technology allowed congregations to continue meeting together via the web. It's hard to imagine having to go through the pandemic without YouTube and Zoom and Facebook Live. What so many people use for sin, God uses for good.

You may say, "But, Amir, technology isn't my thing. Nobody cares about what I say. If I ever post anything, I get six likes at most—four of which are usually family." Technology is *a* thing for spreading the gospel; it is not *the* thing. What has God given to you that you can be faithful with? Maybe God gave you an empathetic personality so that people are drawn to confide in you. Maybe He put you in a work environment that allows you to stand apart from others through your commitment to righteousness and purity. Maybe the Lord has blessed you with location, situating you right next door to that surly neighbor who nobody wants to talk to, yet whose life could be radically transformed through an introduction by you to the joy of the Lord. The church in Philadelphia wasn't affirmed by God for their location; God's kudos came from their faithfulness in using the location that He had given to them. What has God given to you, and are you using it to His glory?

There is one more part of Jesus' statement we must address because it sets us up for the next chapter. In His statement of affirmation and reward, Jesus said, "I also will keep you from the hour of trial which shall come upon the whole world, to test those who dwell on the earth" (Revelation 3:10). What is this trial that is coming upon the world? That is what the rest of the book of Revelation is about. This trial is the tribulation that God is visiting upon this earth to test the Jews and to judge the Gentiles. But what is His promise to the church? "I also will keep you from the hour of trial." That word translated "from" is the Greek word *ek*, and it is one of the most wonderful words that you will ever read. In that little two-letter preposition is God's promise that the church will not have to experience the terror of the coming Day of the Lord.

"But, Amir, Jesus is saying this to one church. How can you say this promise applies to all the church?" In Revelation 1, Jesus mentions the seven churches. Chapters 2 and 3 are all about the church. Once Revelation 4 begins, the church is gone. It is not mentioned again until the return of the bride with Christ at the second coming in Revelation 19. Why? Because chapters 4–19 are all about the "hour of trial," and the church will be taken "out of" that time. We will not be here. We will have been raptured. While the wrath of God is being poured out below, we will be enjoying the wedding of the Son above.

LAODICEA—THE CHURCH
THAT MAKES JESUS SICK

Jesus now completes His cycle of the churches with what is the most disturbing description of all. The city of Laodicea had a problem—it lacked water during the summers when the Lycus River would dry up. An aqueduct was built to bring water in. However, an aqueduct is only as good as its sources. The Laodicean aqueduct drew its water from two places. Nearby was the town of Hierapolis, famed for its hot springs. Further away was the city of Colossae, which was amply supplied by ice-cold mountain runoff. As the life-giving liquid traveled the source aqueducts and eventually merged into one stream, the piping hot and the icy cold combined into a lukewarm blend of *meh* that ran down into the city.

Jesus' words to the church at Laodicea were harsh. "I know your works, that you are neither cold nor hot. I could wish you were cold or hot. So then, because you are lukewarm, and neither cold nor hot, I will vomit you out of My mouth" (Revelation 3:15-16). Not even the mostly dead church of Sardis got such a descriptive admonition. What was it about the Laodiceans that caused the Lord to have such a nauseous response? It appears to be comfort and self-reliance.

Laodicea was a wealthy city known for its banking, its medical school, and its production of luxurious black wool. When an earthquake had all but destroyed the city in AD 60, the merchants were able to rebuild using their own money with no help from Rome. This wealth existed in the church as well. "I am rich, have become wealthy, and have need of nothing" (Revelation 3:17), they said. It is this very attitude that led Jesus to say of the rich young man, "It is easier for a camel to go through the eye of a needle than for a rich man to enter the kingdom of God" (Matthew 19:24). It is need that keeps us on our knees. It is comfort that leads us to wonder, *What do I need God for?*

The Western church is wealthy and comfortable, and, as such, is to a large extent dangerously lukewarm. This is because so many have bought into the world's temporal mindset. Life is all about the material stuff and living in the here and now. It is when our eyes are opened to the spiritual that we see the desperate need in which we are living. How can we keep our eyes on the spiritual so that we don't fall into apathy and complacency—a vomit-inducing lukewarmness? The spiritual perspective will come only as we spend time in the Bible and on our knees in prayer. These tools will aid us in blocking out the worthless and focusing on the priceless.

If you have lost your first love or feel that you have drifted away from God, if you are caught up in a sinful lifestyle or feel that your spiritual walk is stone-cold dead, if you have become apathetic in your walk with Christ and feel that your worship of Him is just empty routine, don't be discouraged. In fact, rejoice that the Holy Spirit has made you aware of these problems. And if you're worried that God is too angry with you to take you back—that maybe He's so fed up with your roller-coaster relationship with Him that He is done with you—then read Jesus' next words:

> Behold, I stand at the door and knock. If anyone hears My voice and opens the door, I will come in to him and dine with him, and he with Me. To him who overcomes I will grant to sit with Me on My throne, as I also overcame and sat down with My Father on His throne (Revelation 3:20-21).

If you've shut Jesus out of your life, fear not. You may have left Him, but He has never left you. He is knocking at the door of your heart. Take some time before you read on to close your eyes and open the door. You won't have to go searching for Him. He will be right there waiting for you to invite Him in so that He can take back control of your life.

CHAPTER 9

ISRAEL IN REVELATION— PART 1

The Arrival of the Day of the Lord

If Revelation were being written by an epic novelist, there would be a page inserted between chapters 3 and 4 with two words boldly printed on it: Book Two. Everything is now different.

As we enter chapter 4, we come to a big shift in time. Chapters 2 and 3 centered on the church as it was in the first century. Jesus affirmed, challenged, and condemned the churches based on their successes, struggles, and sins. Certainly there were elements that were forward-looking, particularly with His repetition of promises of future rewards for those who overcome. There was also a timeless quality to many of Jesus' admonitions and affirmations—words that are as true for the church today as they were for the first-century church. But once chapter 4 begins, John is taken into a time that is yet to come. When Jesus told John, "Write the things which you have seen, and the things which are, and the things which will take place after this" (Revelation 1:19), He made it clear that the disciple's writings will fall into those three categories.

The location shifts as well. We don't know how the time John spent with Jesus on the island of Patmos ended. Was there more conversation between these old friends that is not recorded? Did they maybe share a meal together before parting? It's impossible to know because the written transition is so abrupt. Chapter 1 was written as a narrative; chapters 2 and 3 were letters; now, chapter 4 returns to the narrative, but with a time gap.

REVELATION 4: A JOURNEY TO HEAVEN

John writes, "After these things I looked, and behold, a door standing open in heaven. And the first voice which I heard was like a trumpet speaking with me, saying, 'Come up here, and I will show you things which must take place after this.' Immediately I was in the Spirit; and behold, a throne set in heaven, and One sat on the throne" (Revelation 4:1-2). "These things" is clearly referring to the letter writing, but "after" is an ambiguous term. Was it immediately following? Did time pass? Was it the next day? This was likely not instantly after Jesus dictated to the church of Laodicea the words, "He who has an ear, let him hear what the Spirit says to the churches" (Revelation 3:22) because it is hard to imagine there being no reference to Jesus still being there as the door to heaven opens and John enters into that spiritual realm.

That being said, my words "hard to imagine" are not a precise method of biblical interpretation. As I've mentioned before, there is much in Scripture that is left to the imagination. We grasp with both hands truth that is clearly spelled out. We hold on much more loosely to those areas where we seek to read between the lines. I emphasize this here just to remind you that I will always let you know when what I am telling you falls under the category of "what makes sense to me."

What John describes after he passes through that heavenly door is one of the most magnificent passages in all of Scripture. It is a look into the true Holy of Holies—the place where God Himself dwells. It is a feast for the senses. The apostle's eyes behold "a throne set in heaven, and One sat on the throne. And He who sat there was like a jasper and a sardius stone in appearance; and there was a rainbow around the throne, in appearance like an emerald" (Revelation 4:2-3). And who is the One sitting on that throne? John lets the "four living creatures" do the identifying, saying,

Holy, holy, holy,
Lord God Almighty,
Who was and is and is to come! (verse 8).

The beauty must have been breathtaking. Elders in white robes with golden crowns on their heads, a sea of glass reflecting the surrounding color display like a crystal, four strange eye-covered creatures resembling a lion, a calf, a man, and an eagle, in turn—all amazing. But each of these wonders pales in comparison to the One on the throne whom Daniel had centuries before identified as the "Ancient of Days" (Daniel 7:9). This is the vision that gets my blood racing in anticipation for the first time that I will see my Creator face to face in all His glory! It is just one more reason why I find myself praying, "Even so, come, Lord Jesus!" (Revelation 22:20).

The throne room of God wasn't just a feast for the eyes. John's ears would have been overwhelmed too. "From the throne came flashes of lightning, and rumblings and peals of thunder" (Revelation 4:5 ESV). The Greek word translated "rumblings" is the word for voices, but it can also be used for the sounds made by wind or wings or musical instruments. Suffice it to say that between the claps of thunder and whatever this other great noise was, the throne room was not a quiet place. But then voices came cutting through the cacophony. First, the chanting of the four creatures that we read in verse 8. Then, in response, the words of the twenty-four elders as they cast their crowns down before the throne of God, saying,

You are worthy, O Lord,
To receive glory and honor and power;
For You created all things,
And by Your will they exist and were created
    (Revelation 4:11).

There is one more sound that carries through the throne room—music. It isn't until chapter 5 that John tips us off to this detail. At the time the Lamb takes the scroll, John writes, "Now when He had taken the scroll, the four living creatures and the twenty-four elders fell down before the Lamb, each having a harp, and golden bowls full of incense, which are the prayers of the saints" (Revelation 5:8). Because the golden bowls seem to fulfill a purpose—holding the incense of the prayers of the saints—there is no reason to believe the harps are simply props. Instead, this is a twenty-four-piece harp ensemble playing melodious hymns of worship for the Lord God.

We also discover in that same verse one more of John's senses that likely went into overload—his sense of smell. Each of the elders holds a bowl, and each bowl is filled with incense. I have taken many tour groups to the Church of the Nativity in Bethlehem. After descending a set of stairs, one comes to the place where tradition holds that Mary gave birth to Jesus. It is a fairly small space with only a limited number of people able to fit in at any given time. There have been occasions when I have had groups down there and the church's Orthodox priests have descended the stairs with their incense censers swinging in their hands. The smoke fills the room, giving it a wonderful, heady aroma. To me, that is the fragrance of the throne room of our Lord.

There is one other shift that takes place from chapters 2 and 3 to chapter 4—that is a focus shift. The previous chapters were written directly to and about the church. Chapter 4 has the same recipients— the first-century churches—but the narrative now turns to the Jews and the fallen world. From Revelation 4:1 all the way to the middle of chapter 19, the church is never mentioned. Why? Because the church is no longer here on earth. It is not included in the description of the events that will happen in this world. It is not referenced at all in the narrative.

The reason for this is that included in John's words "After these things…" in verse 1 is the rapture of the church from earth. Those three words mark the end the church age and open the door to the Day of the Lord—it is here the focus turns back to God's original chosen people. This is not the church's tribulation; it is the Jews' period of testing. What other reason could there be for the church to be utterly absent from the coming time of wrath? This was not an oversight on John's part. He didn't get so wrapped up in describing the coming events that mentioning the church's role in the tribulation just slipped his mind.

The church is not mentioned because the church is gone—raptured—having met the Savior in the clouds. And the church will go with Him to His heavenly realm, where the Lord had ascended to so many years ago to prepare a place for those of us who have made Him our Lord and Savior.

REVELATION 5:
THE LION AND THE LAMB

Now that the scene has been set, the action begins. "I saw in the right hand of Him who sat on the throne a scroll written inside and on the back, sealed with seven seals. Then I saw a strong angel proclaiming with a loud voice, 'Who is worthy to open the scroll and to loose its seals?' And no one in heaven or on the earth or under the earth was able to open the scroll, or to look at it" (Revelation 5:1-3). The Ancient of Days held forth a document, rolled and held shut by seven seals. An excited sense of anticipation would have passed through all those who surrounded the throne, including John. What had the hand of God written? What wisdom was about to be revealed or mystery explained? Because of the importance of this great scroll—one containing so much information that, contrary to standard practice, it had been written upon on both sides—it could not be opened by some ordinary herald. Only one who was perfect could open the perfect revelation of the Father. An angel cried out for one worthy to come forward. John looked around, wondering who this great personage might be. But as his eyes scanned the throne room, he was greatly disappointed.

No one came forward. No sooner had the action started than it came to a screeching halt. Even in the presence of the Almighty God, there was no one worthy to read or even look at the contents of this singular document. John's heart was broken. He wept before the God who had promised to end all sorrow.

But then, in the midst of his grief, John heard a voice calling to him. He looked up and saw one of the elders beckoning him. If a man on a throne tells you to come, it's usually best you come. So John crossed to where this white-clad, newly crownless man was seated. "Do not weep. Behold, the Lion of the tribe of Judah, the Root of David, has prevailed to open the scroll and to loose its seven seals" (verse 5). Following the man's pointed finger, John turned and was stunned by what he saw. Here we find one of the great juxtapositions of Scripture. The elder indicated to John the approach of a great Lion, and the apostle turned to discover a bloody Lamb. Here, we find a perfect picture of the character of Jesus Christ.

Jesus is the Lion of Judah. He is the all-powerful Creator of all things (John 1:1-3; Colossians 1:15-16), the Judge of all mankind (Acts 10:42), and the Bringer of Wrath in the last days (Revelation 19:11-16). This is a very different understanding of Jesus for those who focus only on the popular depictions of Jesus as the sweet little manger-baby, meek and mild, or as the wise, soft-spoken teacher whose only goal is for everyone to love everyone else. Because of these one-sided viewpoints, there are many biblically ignorant teachers and activists and pastors and denominations who claim Jesus doesn't really care that much about antiquated morality, especially when it comes to who does what with whom. They ignore the lionesque nature of the Warrior Savior, forgetting that when Jesus took on flesh, it was not in place of His justice, righteousness, and truth.

But if Jesus were all lion, He would be a fearful Lord—One destined to be honored and obeyed, but not necessarily loved. Enter the sacrificial Lamb. If you want a visual of the amazing perfection of the character of our Savior, you need only to turn to John 13. In the upper room, Jesus—God Himself—knelt before His disciples and one by one washed the dirt and muck of first-century roads off their feet. That includes the grimy toes of each disciple—even those of the one who that same night would betray Him. It's hard to not get emotional picturing this scene. Later that evening, after Judas Iscariot had departed to carry out his treacherous task, Jesus in one word communicated His motivation for what He had done for the disciples and what He was about to do on the cross for the world—love. It was His love for them, and His desire for them to emulate that same love toward others, that inspired the foot-washing. He said, "As the

Father loved Me, I also have loved you; abide in My love...This is My commandment, that you love one another as I have loved you. Greater love has no one than this, than to lay down one's life for his friends" (John 15:9,12-13).

Jesus is the Lion and the Lamb—One to be feared and loved, One who desires obedience and relationship, One who will judge people for their sins, yet has sacrificed Himself on the cross to take away that same judgment. As John watched, the Savior—still bearing the bloody marks of His crucifixion—walked to the throne of the Almighty Father and took the scroll from His right hand.

And the place erupted!

The four creatures and the elders all dropped to the ground as incense smoke poured forth from the elders' golden bowls. Singing and music filled the air in celebration of the Lamb:

> You are worthy to take the scroll,
> And to open its seals;
> For You were slain,
> And have redeemed us to God by Your blood
> Out of every tribe and tongue and people and nation,
> And have made us kings and priests to our God,
> And we shall reign on the earth (Revelation 5:9-10).

Soon a choir of thousands upon thousands of angels took up the chorus, joining with the creatures and the elders to sing the praises of the risen Savior:

> Worthy is the Lamb who was slain
> To receive power and riches and wisdom,
> And strength and honor and glory and blessing! (verse 12).

How I envy John being able to witness this impromptu worship service. He must have stood there with his mouth open as tears filled his eyes—tears this time not from sorrow, but from joy and wonder and amazement at the splendor of the moment. But sadly, it was just for a moment, because once the praise wound down, the Lamb set to work on the seals and the mood changed completely.

REVELATION 6:
THE BEGINNING OF TROUBLES

"Now I saw when the Lamb opened one of the seals; and I heard one of the four living creatures saying with a voice like thunder, 'Come and see.' And I looked, and behold, a white horse. He who sat on it had a bow; and a crown was given to him, and he went out conquering and to conquer" (Revelation 6:1-2). With those words, the judgment of God began. The Lamb initiated the seal judgments by breaking the first of the seals affixed to the scroll. Immediately one of the four strange creatures surrounding the throne of the Almighty cried out, "Come." A warrior came galloping on a great white steed—the first of what have come to be known as the four horsemen of the apocalypse. The rider was handed a crown to show that he was on a mission to rule on the earth. This was likely the Antichrist going forth to establish his authority on the earth.

Three more seals were broken one by one, and John witnessed similar scenes. The second seal brought a fiery red horse. The rider was handed a large sword, and he galloped forth to bring war amongst the nations. The third seal was separated from the scroll, and a black horse came forward. This rider, with his scales representing scarcity and mass inflation, was tasked with bringing famine and shortage.

With the fourth seal, it's easy to sense a mood change. Maybe the air chilled a bit and the smell of decay cut through the incense. This time there were not one, but two riders. The first rode a foul horse the greenish-grey pallor of something that had long since died. This was apropos because the rider on its back was Death. Hades followed behind, acting as his wingman. Death's mission was to kill, and on a massive scale. "Power was given to them over a fourth of the earth, to kill with sword, with hunger, with death, and by the beasts of the earth" (Revelation 6:8).

The current world population is 7.8 billion.[8] If we subtract out the estimated 619 million evangelical Christians[9] who have already been raptured when the seals are broken, we are left with approximately 7.2 billion people. This means that when Death and Hades complete their initial mission, 1.8 billion people will have been wiped out. Compare that to the hundreds of thousands who have died due to the coronavirus.

I'm not discounting the devastation of the pandemic. Instead, I'm emphasizing the massive toll that will be taken on the world.

War, starvation, disease, and wild animals will all share in the slaughter. That last one is interesting. The parts of the earth where there is currently mortal danger from animals are few. The fact that death by lions and tigers and bears and other predators will take place on a massive scale indicates a breakdown in society that causes either a major decrease in the animals' natural food supply or an ease of access to human prey—or both. Either way, I'm going to take a moment right now to thank God once again that I won't be on earth as the seals are being opened.

Before we see what happens when the last three seals are broken, it would be beneficial to look once again at why this is taking place. There are two reasons that God brings this great tribulation upon the earth. One is to bring a final punishment upon those who have rejected His grace and mercy. This is the just recompense for their sin. Paul wrote, "The wages of sin is death, but the gift of God is eternal life in Christ Jesus our Lord" (Romans 6:23). All face the decision to either choose death or choose life. Those who turn their backs on the free gift of salvation have earned their punishment. That is why Paul said that death is the wages—or the payment—for sin.

The Lord does not want anyone to go through the tribulation, which is why it is still yet to begin. But His patience will come to an end.

> The Lord is not slack concerning His promise, as some count slackness, but is longsuffering toward us, not willing that any should perish but that all should come to repentance. But the day of the Lord will come as a thief in the night, in which the heavens will pass away with a great noise, and the elements will melt with fervent heat; both the earth and the works that are in it will be burned up (2 Peter 3:9-10).

Once the church is removed from the earth, those left behind will physically experience the penalty for how they lived their lives.

There is another reason for the tribulation. It is similar to the first in that there will be a righteously severe price paid for sin. However, in this second case, there is a light at the end of the tunnel. For the Gentile world, the seven years will end with a period—or maybe an exclamation mark. When it's done, it's done. For the Jew, however, the end of the tribulation is a comma because their story will continue. The Gentile reason for the tribulation is punishment; the Jewish reason is discipline. They are two similar concepts, but with very different purposes.

The Gentile reason for the tribulation is
punishment; the Jewish reason is discipline.

With punishment, one pays for what they have done. With discipline, one still walks through a difficult time, yet the goal of the struggle is repentance, growth, and righteousness. There is the promise of ultimate reconciliation. That reconciliation of the Father to His wife, Israel, is the greater purpose of the seven years of woe. Jeremiah gave this period a very telling name when he wrote, "Alas! For that day is great, so that none is like it; and it is the time of Jacob's trouble, but he shall be saved out of it" (Jeremiah 30:7). This verse tells us both what the tribulation is and why it is. God has established His plan of seals, trumpets, and bowls for the sake of Jacob—whom He renamed Israel (Genesis 32:28)—and He has done this so that ultimately, there could come the salvation of His people.

Again, notice that it is the time of Jacob's trouble. It is not the time of the church's trouble. The church will be gone, while Israel remains.

Sadly, salvation will not come for all of God's chosen people. In that time, many Jews will die in their sins along with the Gentiles.

> "It shall come to pass in all the land,"
>   Says the LORD,
> "That two-thirds in it shall be cut off and die,
>   But one-third shall be left in it:
>   I will bring the one-third through the fire,

Will refine them as silver is refined,
And test them as gold is tested.
They will call on My name,
And I will answer them.
I will say, 'This is My people';
And each one will say, 'The LORD is my God'"
  (Zechariah 13:8-9).

Two-thirds of the Jews will be wiped out. That's devastating. I can picture so many of the people that I see each and every day in my neighborhood or when I travel to Jerusalem. To know that they will die without ever knowing the truth of the Messiah who sacrificed Himself for them is a difficult concept to even contemplate. However, I also take heart in the fact that one out of three who today reject Jesus as Savior will be singing and dancing and celebrating as they watch me and the rest of the church return with our Lord to the Mount of Olives. What a day of rejoicing that will be!

Punishment for the unbelievers. Discipline for the Jews. What reason is there for the church to endure the tribulation? None. Some postulate that it is for the purification of the church, but if we could purify ourselves, then what reason is there for the cross? There is no possibility of perfection for us while still on this earth—only varying degrees of imperfection. We've already been washed by the blood of Christ so that when God looks at us, He sees us as righteous. For those who see the church as replacing Israel, you're welcome to your time in Jacob's trouble. For me, I'll pass. I've got a wedding to get to.

With the opening of the fifth seal, we are offered a bittersweet revelation: "When He opened the fifth seal, I saw under the altar the souls of those who had been slain for the word of God and for the testimony which they held" (Revelation 6:9). Taking refuge under the heavenly altar were the souls of Christians killed during the tribulation. Often referred to as tribulation saints, these will be the men and women who realized too late that the gospel they had heard from their mother or their neighbor or their coworker was true after all. Receiving Christ as their Savior during the tribulation, they were then killed for their faith.

Why is this bittersweet? It is bitter in that they will be martyred for their faith. It is sweet because it shows that there is still hope for the salvation of our loved ones after the rapture. The likelihood of post-rapture salvation may not be great because the spirit of deception in the world will be powerful with the Antichrist. However, it is obvious that, by the time the fifth seal is broken, repentance and reconciliation can still happen.

We should notice two things about these saints. First, they are separate from the church. When they reach heaven, they will not be ushered into their heavenly mansions. Instead, traumatized by their ordeal, they will be given white robes and told to rest until the full number has come in of their brothers and sisters who will be killed for Christ (Revelation 6:11). Second, they are simply souls. They will not have been given the resurrection bodies that those in the church will already be enjoying. Their opportunity for transformation will have to wait until later.

The sixth seal will open to devastation on a climactic scale:

> I looked when He opened the sixth seal, and behold, there was a great earthquake; and the sun became black as sack-cloth of hair, and the moon became like blood. And the stars of heaven fell to the earth, as a fig tree drops its late figs when it is shaken by a mighty wind. Then the sky receded as a scroll when it is rolled up, and every mountain and island was moved out of its place (Revelation 6:12-14).

While it is very easy to read a nuclear holocaust into this passage, we need to be careful to keep our lines between speculation and knowledge strong. Could this be a great nuclear event? It certainly could, and it would fit well with seals one through four. However, it is also just as possible that this is exactly as it reads—a great earthquake, smoke and ash blocking out the sun, and meteors or other nonterrestrial objects showering down from the sky. What we do know for sure is that its effect will be so horrifying that people—from great to small—will be praying that they would just die rather than have to endure any more wrath.

REVELATION 7:
TRIBULATION EVANGELISM

From here onward, we will move a little more rapidly through Revelation. As much as I would love to break down each event, that is not the ultimate purpose of this book. Rather than create an analytical commentary, my goal is for you to come away with a feel for the flow and to see God's distinct Israel-directed purpose. Many are nervous about reading too deeply into Revelation, or they end up getting lost in some of the seemingly confusing details. My hope is to take away some of the mystery that some people may find off-putting so that this wonderful and essential portion of the Bible becomes more accessible. In the near future, I will be releasing a study commentary on the book of Revelation that will go into much more detail.

John's writings are narrative in nature. In other words, he related all that he saw. His narration is linear in that he wrote of the events as they were revealed to him. However, his timeline is not always chronological. John wrote as he saw what was revealed to him, but God was not always showing the activities in the order that they will happen. In Revelation 7, we have a pause in the opening of the seals. In this break we are introduced to two great congregations of people.

First, we meet the 144,000 witnesses—12,000 from each tribe of Israel. Their purpose will be to spread the gospel of Jesus Christ to those suffering through the tribulation. Imagine 144,000 young Jewish Billy Grahams traveling from nation to nation, pleading for people to turn from their sin and rebellion and put their hope in Jesus Christ. I can't help but get excited when I read about these passionate young men. I love that, like myself, they are Jews who have discovered the identity of the true Messiah. John calls them the "firstfruits to God and to the Lamb" (Revelation 14:4). As firstfruits, they will be set aside and offered up to God as the first of what will ultimately be the salvation of all Israel at the second coming of Christ (Romans 11:26).

I can picture in my mind this evangelistic force. Young men, the age of my older son, fired up for Christ—throwing all the passion and energy they now have for the things of this world into spreading the gospel. While my son will not be one of them—he will be with me in heaven with Christ—I do know many of his friends. If the 144,000 are anything like them, they will be a formidable evangelistic force.

The second group we meet are those who are the product of the work of the 144,000. A "great multitude which no one could number, of all nations, tribes, peoples, and tongues, standing before the throne and before the Lamb, clothed with white robes, with palm branches in their hands" (Revelation 7:9). For the reader, this is not an introduction but a reacquaintance. We have already met this multitude at the sixth seal. These are the tribulation saints who were hidden under the altar and were given clean white robes. Now we see them having donned those robes, and, instead of pleading for judgment against their persecutors, they are singing a song of praise to God: "Salvation belongs to our God who sits on the throne, and to the Lamb!" (verse 10). Sorrow will turn to praise when we enter the throne room of our great God!

Once the church is taken away, the responsibility of pointing the world to God will return to Israel. Two peoples, two roles—both loved and used by God.

Before we move on, please notice the identity of the primary evangelists of the tribulation. It is not the church. God had to look elsewhere to find His workforce. Why? Because the church is gone. His chosen sealed-with-the-Spirit servants are already with Him in heaven, so He turns to His original chosen servants and seals them on their foreheads (verse 3). Israel was the first who were given the role of being a light to the nations. When they rejected their mission, the assignment was passed on to the church. Once the church is taken away, the responsibility of pointing the world to God will return to Israel. Two peoples, two roles—both loved and used by God.

REVELATION 8:
ECOLOGICAL DISASTERS

Silence. The Lamb opened the seventh seal, and John waited for a horse or an earthquake or something. But all was still. How eerie it must have been, the anticipation permeating the air. Finally, after thirty minutes went by, there was movement. John watched as trumpets were passed out to the seven angels who stood next to the throne. Then a large amount of incense was given to the angel that manned (angelled) the altar of incense, and the smoke began to rise and fill the room. Everything was still calm, but all who were present were on the edge of their seats.

Then John must have gasped when suddenly the angel by the altar flew into motion. Taking hold of an incense burner, he filled it with fire from the altar and hurled it to the earth. Smoke trailed behind it as it sailed through the atmosphere and crashed to the ground. An electrical storm erupted and an earthquake shook the ground. This ominous sign foreshadowed the devastation that was about to take place—ecological disaster on a grand scale.

The first angel blew his trumpet and fires raged over a third of the earth. The second trumpet sounded and a massive rock—possibly a fiery meteor—crashed into the sea, killing a third of the sea life and wiping out a third of all shipping with the resulting tsunami. Another possible meteor, or maybe a nuclear missile, fell on the earth at the third trumpet blast, tainting a third of all fresh waters. When the sound of the fourth trumpet echoed through heaven, a celestial calamity of some sort took place that affected the sun and moon and stars.

By the end of the first four trumpets, the earth was reeling. Global warming and climate change were forgotten. People wondered how the earth could possibly survive the beating that it had taken.

But there were still three trumpets yet to sound.

REVELATION 9: A HUMAN HOLOCAUST

The description of what happens when the fifth trumpet sounds is very disturbing. Out of a great, smoking abyss came an army of locusts.

It was not an army of death, but of agony. They flew out across the earth in search of people to torture. Intentionally avoiding the Jews and Gentiles who had become Christians but were not yet martyred, they attacked all others in order to "torment them for five months. Their torment was like the torment of a scorpion when it strikes a man. In those days men will seek death and will not find it; they will desire to die, and death will flee from them" (Revelation 9:5-6). How John's heart must have ached as he witnessed the misery of the unbelieving masses.

After the sixth angel blew his trumpet, he released four other angels who had been waiting at the river Euphrates. These angels of death had been bound there for who knows how long for this very moment when they would be set loose on the world. When they were freed, carnage followed. One-third of all humanity was slaughtered.

Back to the math: We had already lost 1.8 billion people to the hand of the pale rider when the fourth seal was broken. That left us with 5.4 billion remaining. Even though many more will have perished through the trumpet judgments, let's continue to use that number as our baseline. Losing a third—or another 1.8 billion—to the four avenging angels means that at least half of the world's 7.2 billion people will have died by the end of the sixth trumpet. That's more than 3.5 billion souls. It's hard to even imagine.

When we write off sin in our lives or the lives of others as no big deal, we need to remember this mind-boggling number. Sin is rebellion against the Creator. It is expressing to Him that we are going to do things our way and not His. It is telling Him that we are our own god, and He can take His Bible and His rules and go pound sand. Sin—no matter how big or small—matters.

This number is also a reminder of what we owe to our Savior. In spite of every person's arrogant rejection of God, Jesus still died for us. It is because of His love and His sacrifice that we are offered the glorious opportunity to escape being one of those 3.5 billion wiped out by God's wrath—or, maybe worse yet, being one of those who survive.

CHAPTER 10

ISRAEL IN REVELATION— PART 2

The End of the Old and the Beginning of the New

As we enter Revelation 10, John is brought back into the narrative. Rather than simply watching, he once again participates in the events.

REVELATION 10: A BITTERSWEET MOMENT

At the opening of the chapter, a magnificent angel left heaven for earth:

> I saw still another mighty angel coming down from heaven, clothed with a cloud. And a rainbow was on his head, his face was like the sun, and his feet like pillars of fire. He had a little book open in his hand. And he set his right foot on the sea and his left foot on the land, and cried with a loud voice, as when a lion roars. When he cried out, seven thunders uttered their voices (Revelation 10:1-3).

The arrival and call of this great spiritual being prompted the seven thunders to cry out their own message. John was about to write the words of the thunders when a voice called from heaven and told him to keep their statement to himself.

But John didn't have time to stow his writing kit because the action kept right on going. The great angel reached his hand up to where John was in heaven, swearing by God and His creation that the mysteries of this great Day of the Lord that had been declared to the prophets so long ago were about to be completed.

The voice from heaven called again to John and told him to go and take a book from the upstretched hand of the mighty angel. As John did so, the angel said to him, "Take and eat it; and it will make your stomach bitter, but it will be as sweet as honey in your mouth" (verse 9). As strange as this is for us to hear, for John it likely spurred a little flutter in his insides. This leader of the church knew the Scriptures—from his early education as a young Jew to the decades he had spent as a leader of God's church. When he was told to eat this book, his mind would have immediately gone to the prophet Ezekiel's experience:

> Now when I looked, there was a hand stretched out to me; and behold, a scroll of a book was in it. Then He spread it before me; and there was writing on the inside and on the outside, and written on it were lamentations and mourning and woe. Moreover He said to me, "Son of man, eat what you find; eat this scroll, and go, speak to the house of Israel." So I opened my mouth, and He caused me to eat that scroll. And He said to me, "Son of man, feed your belly, and fill your stomach with this scroll that I give you." So I ate, and it was in my mouth like honey in sweetness (Ezekiel 2:9–3:3).

A scroll written upon inside and out was held forth by a hand for a chronicler to take and eat. John was now being asked to do the same thing. When Ezekiel ate the scroll, his action served as a picture affirming that the words that the prophet spoke were coming from the Lord. The Word of God was now inside of him, and from that source,

Ezekiel would prophesy. John was now given this same affirmation. He ingested the sweetness of the words of the Lord, but in his case, what he ingested didn't sit well with him. What was about to happen to the Jews and the unbelievers was so horrific—so devastating—that its truth burned in his stomach.

Like John, we are able to "ingest" the Word of God, and it is sweet and delicious. In this way we learn about who our God is and His desire for us to be with Him. We discover and accept the great plan of salvation that comes through Jesus' sacrifice on the cross. We "taste and see that the LORD is good" (Psalm 34:8). Yet when we take time to think about our loved ones and friends and neighbors who will endure the judgments of the seals and trumpets and bowls, it should cause our stomachs to sour. We know the terrible ramifications of rejecting God's beautiful truth, and it should motivate us to be diligent in sharing what has been revealed to us in Scripture—the same way that John was so passionately motivated to share what God revealed directly to him.

God's grace knows no bounds. Even in this time of punishment and discipline, the Lord continues to call people to repentance.

REVELATION 11: JERUSALEM'S PREACHERS AND EARTHQUAKE

God's grace knows no bounds. Even in this time of punishment and discipline, the Lord continues to call people to repentance. It is important to never lose sight of the heart of the Lord in the midst of Revelation. As Peter said, God is "not willing that any should perish but that all should come to repentance" (2 Peter 3:9). To that end, He first sent 144,000 to take the gospel around the world. Now we see Him adding two more witnesses into the mix, and this pair is unique.

From Jerusalem, these two men preached their message of accusation and warning. They spoke of the hope that is found in Jesus and the utter lack of hope for those without Him. Like the prophets of old, they told people what they didn't want to hear—that they are sinners, and the punishment for their sin is now upon them. As the population around the world watched these two men on their televisions, their anger for them grew. Having seen the violent riots of 2020 that took place in the United States and Europe and the Middle East, it is not difficult to picture the tumultuous scene around these two individuals. A mob that was filled with bullhorns and vile chants and obscene gestures would surround them and press closer and closer. Then when some black-masked thug inevitably lashed out at them, the crowd would be met with a terrible surprise. When attacked, "fire proceeds from their mouth and devours their enemies. And if anyone wants to harm them, he must be killed in this manner" (Revelation 11:5).

It will likely take only a few attempts on the lives of these men for people to clue in that they had better keep their hands off. However, that doesn't mean they will listen to these two spokesmen for God. The witnesses will move to Plan B to try to get the people's attention. They will be given the "power to shut heaven, so that no rain falls in the days of their prophecy; and they have power over waters to turn them to blood, and to strike the earth with all plagues, as often as they desire" (verse 6). Yet even with this demonstration of God's power, few will repent.

John then wrote, "When they finish their testimony, the beast that ascends out of the bottomless pit will make war against them, overcome them, and kill them. And their dead bodies will lie in the street of the great city which spiritually is called Sodom and Egypt, where also our Lord was crucified" (verses 7-8). Notice that it wasn't until after they had completed the task God had given to them that the beast overcame them. The beast had no power to stop them from doing God's will. All he could do was overcome them, when God handed them over to him. And even then, the victory remained with God and the witnesses.

"Now after the three-and-a-half days the breath of life from God entered them, and they stood on their feet, and great fear fell on those who saw them. And they heard a loud voice from heaven saying to them, 'Come up here.' And they ascended to heaven in a cloud, and their enemies saw them" (verses 11-12). After three days, they were raised, just like Jesus. Then they ascended to heaven, just like Jesus. And, if the people weren't reeling enough after these events, a devastating earthquake immediately hit Jerusalem, destroying a tenth of the city.

REVELATION 12:
THE NATION THAT WON'T DIE

Israel is the nation that will not die—no matter how hard other nations have tried to wipe it out in the past. The continued existence of the Jews is testimony to the power and plan of an Almighty God. In this chapter, the Lord shows His plan—past and future—for His people. Why? Because their eventual salvation is the primary purpose for this entire earth-shaking period.

In Revelation 12, as John watched, an interesting sign appeared in heaven. He saw a woman, a child, and a dragon. The woman represented Israel, the child was Jesus, and the dragon was Satan. The dragon attempted to devour the child, who had just been born to the woman. But the child, Jesus, was "snatched up" to heaven. In other words, Satan attempted to put an end to Jesus by leading the Jews and Romans to crucify the "child." But Jesus was raised from the dead and ascended back to His home in heaven. Meanwhile, the woman, Israel, was protected in the desert for three and a half years.

This divine protection can be seen in the fact that we Jews are still alive after 2,000 years of the devil's attempts to destroy us during the church age. However, the passage also speaks of a very specific number of days that Israel, as a nation, will be protected in the desert. The desert, in this context, is a literal desert—a rocky, sandy, barren place. And the time is a literal time—three-and-one-half years.

In speaking of the relationship between the Antichrist and Israel during the seven years of the tribulation, Daniel said, "He shall confirm a covenant with many for one week; but in the middle of the week he shall bring an end to sacrifice and offering. And on the wing of abominations shall be one who makes desolate, even until the con-summation, which is determined, is poured out on the desolate" (Dan-iel 9:27). The Hebrew word translated "confirm" is *hegbir*, and it means more than just to "agree" or "make." Those words are too static. Instead, the word is forward-looking and has the idea of "increase." If I were to ask one of my children to turn up the volume on the television, I would use the word *hegbir*.

This is true of the confirming of the covenant with the Antichrist. The love and admiration that the Jews have for the beast will increase for the first half of the week, or three-and-one-half years. Peace will reign. But then the Antichrist will show himself for who he truly is. The Jews will realize this man is not the Messiah. They'll understand that they have been deceived, and they will flee Jerusalem for the duration of the tribulation. This second three-and-one-half years is what John saw in this vision, when God will protect His people because He is not done with them yet.

REVELATION 13:
ANTICHRIST ONE AND TWO

Popular movie depictions of the Antichrist show him as a fright-ening, sinister personage—part man, part devil. But that's just Holly-wood at its biblically ignorant worst. Even the devil knows that you catch more people with honey than with vinegar. He knows that to draw the naïve in with his deceptions, he must disguise himself as "an angel of light" (2 Corinthians 11:14). This is the same tactic he uses with his minion, the Antichrist.

At this time, John saw two beasts. The first beast—one coming up out of the sea—did not proceed to go forth and terrorize the world. He was not all horns and hooves and pitchfork and spiky tail. Instead, he was all personality and charisma. People were attracted to him. Follow-ing the miraculous healing of a head wound he received, he poured on the charm and the world bought in. "All the world marveled and fol-lowed the beast. So they worshiped the dragon who gave authority to the beast; and they worshiped the beast, saying, 'Who is like the beast?

Who is able to make war with him?'" (Revelation 13:3-4). For forty-two months—three-and-one-half years—this Antichrist accepted the praise and adoration of the nations, including, as we just saw, Israel.

As John continued to watch the scene unfold, a second beast appeared—this one coming up out of the earth. This beast, really a second antichrist, is called the false prophet. Just like a true prophet points people to the true God, the false prophet will point people to a false god:

> He exercises all the authority of the first beast in his presence, and causes the earth and those who dwell in it to worship the first beast, whose deadly wound was healed. He performs great signs, so that he even makes fire come down from heaven on the earth in the sight of men. And he deceives those who dwell on the earth by those signs which he was granted to do in the sight of the beast, telling those who dwell on the earth to make an image to the beast who was wounded by the sword and lived (verses 12-14).

It is also this second beast who will take control of the global financial system. In order to buy or sell anything, a person must receive a mark on the right hand or on the forehead. The mark is the beast's name and is represented numerically—666. At one time the idea of some sort of worldwide individual indicator being used in commerce seemed outlandish, or at least some great mystery, but today, that is no longer true. Personal digital chip technology is already available. Commerce has begun moving from cash to credit cards and it is now progressing to our phones. It will not be long before the next logical step toward personal imbedded identifier chips is made.[10]

REVELATION 14:
EVANGELISM EXPLOSION

In November 1942, after many defeats, the British forces finally scored their first major victory, turning back Nazi general field marshal Erwin Rommel and his army of Panzer tanks. This military win prompted British prime minister Winston Churchill to address the House of Commons with guarded optimism. He said to them, "Now this is not the end. It is not even the beginning of the end. But it is, perhaps, the end of the beginning."[11] When John's narrative stepped away from the trumpet judgments at the conclusion of Revelation 9, that was the end of the beginning of God's wrath being poured out on His creation. Here in chapter 14, we now find ourselves at the beginning of the end.

This starts positively enough with a look back at the 144,000 evangelists. Here they are identified as the "firstfruits to God and to the Lamb" (Revelation 14:4). What joy there is in knowing that there will be an "evangelism explosion" during the tribulation as a result of these men pouring forth the gospel of salvation. Even though it will be extremely difficult to be a Christian during this time—with most suffering martyrdom—we can rejoice that the beast and his followers will only be able to touch the physical bodies of these tribulation saints. Their souls will be safe with their Savior.

Next, a voice called to John from heaven with a very ominous message. Reminiscent of Paul's message "To me, to live is Christ, and to die is gain" (Philippians 1:21), this voice commanded John, "Write: 'Blessed are the dead who die in the Lord from now on.' 'Yes,' says the Spirit, 'that they may rest from their labors, and their works follow them'" (Revelation 14:13). For the tribulation saints, living will mean suffering and misery. But it will also mean the possibility of drawing others into the kingdom of God. And martyrdom will mean rest from the pain.

I believe that we all have the ability to endure suffering and persecution given that three conditions are true: first, we know it is only for a time; second, we are accomplishing something worthwhile; third, there is a reward at the end. This was true of Paul. He knew that a time was coming when his life would end. The pain and persecution he endured would not last into eternity. Also, he was accomplishing something worthwhile, knowing that he would see "fruit from [his] labor" (Philippians 1:22) for as long as he remained on this earth. Finally, he was certain that when he finally departed this life, he would "be with

Christ" (1:23), which he readily admitted would be "far better." That time would come, but it was not yet.

The tribulation saints will know and understand that there is a time limit to the Day of the Lord. Either their lives will be taken, or they will witness the second coming of Christ. But in the meantime, they will be spreading the gospel, using their remaining time on this earth in the most important and productive way possible. All the while, they will know that their reward one day will be to see their Savior face to face and to spend eternity in His presence. If you think about it, there is no difference between their situation and ours, except that they will be serving the Lord in a world that is being systematically taken apart and is about to get much worse.

REVELATION 15: THE PAUSE THAT REFRESHES

This is a chapter of preparation and praise. It is a deep breath before the final series of judgments commence. John saw before him a sea of glass shimmering with fiery reflections. On that glass stood a choir of tribulation saints—harp in hand, ready to praise their God. Interestingly, John described these saints as those who "have the victory over the beast" (Revelation 15:2). One might think, "Wait—these people are all dead. How is this victory?" We must remember that ultimate victory is found not in the physical realm, but the spiritual. The beast may have taken their bodies, but their eternal souls are secure in the presence of their God.

This is why they will be able to break forth in song:

> Great and marvelous are Your works,
> Lord God Almighty!
> Just and true are Your ways,
> O King of the saints!
> Who shall not fear You, O Lord, and glorify Your name?
> For You alone are holy.
> For all nations shall come and worship before You,
> For Your judgments have been manifested (verses 3-4).

As we watch what happens next, it is important to remember the words of these saints: "Just and true are Your ways." God only acts righteously. While we may cringe or even weep at the destruction that is about to descend upon the earth, we must remember that it is completely justified and proper. As we read John's description about the seven bowls being passed out to seven angels, we must keep in mind that the wrath contained in those bowls is deserved and right.

REVELATION 16:
THE ROAD TO ARMAGEDDON

This is one of the saddest and most tragic chapters in the Bible. The final set of judgments—the bowl judgments—will be released to devastate the earth's ecology and people's physical bodies. It is the judgments from these bowls that will pave the road to the final great battle of Armageddon.

The first five bowls were poured out, one after the other. First, horrendous boils broke out on those who had the mark of the beast. Then came the destruction of all sea life, followed by the poisoning of all the water. The fourth bowl brought a scorching heat from the sun. When the people cried out in misery, the Lord took the sun away from them, plunging the earth into absolute, claustrophobic darkness.

Do the people of the earth finally get a clue and repent? They do anything but. After the fourth bowl, they "blasphemed the name of God who has power over these plagues; and they did not repent and give Him glory" (Revelation 16:9). Then, in the midst of the darkness and pain of the fifth bowl, they again "blasphemed the God of heaven because of their pains and their sores, and did not repent of their deeds" (verse 11). There is going to be such spiritual blindness and brainwashing that they will not turn to God. Rather than repent, they will blaspheme. This utter hatred of the Lord will move the kings of the earth to gather to make war against Him in His holy city. Demonic spirits will "go out to the kings of the earth and of the whole world, to gather them to the battle of that great day of God Almighty…And they gathered them together to the place called in Hebrew, Armageddon" (verses 14,16).

Armageddon. This is the only place in Scripture where we read this word. It is, in reality, a beautiful place that receives a bad rap because of what will one day take place there. My house looks out into this lush fertile region—also known as the Valley of Jezreel. It is a wonder to think that one day, the armies of the world will gather out beyond my porch in preparation to march to Jerusalem—sixty miles south—for the great battle.

When the seventh bowl was poured out, the destruction was great. A massive earthquake shook the world, changing the geography and destroying Babylon. This was followed by a hailstorm that dropped 100-pound stones, obliterating countless people and animals and structures. Again, what was the response? "Men blasphemed God because of the plague of the hail, since that plague was exceedingly great" (16:21).

Imagine living through this. If you think living through the coronavirus is misery enough, it is nothing compared to what is to come. Remember, these are not just hypotheticals. This is not figurative language. These are actual events that will happen to actual people. Can you picture your parent or spouse or child going through these miseries? Does this not motivate you to do all you can to make sure they understand how they can avoid the wrath of God by accepting His free gift of grace?

There is one positive that we can cull from this chapter of misery. When John sees the seventh angel pour out his bowl, he hears a voice from heaven—the voice of God on His throne—call out one simple word: "*Gegonen!*" Translated, this Greek word means "It is done!" With the seventh bowl, the wrath of God upon the earth will be satisfied. While spiritual judgment still remains, the physical price is paid.

REVELATION 17–18:
COLLAPSE OF THE WORLDWIDE RELIGION AND BANKRUPTCY OF THE WORLD ECONOMY

These are the only two chapters that we will unite because they go hand in hand. Here is where we find the final fall of Babylon. Through much of Scripture, Babylon is set up as the antithesis to Jerusalem. It is a center of idol worship; Jerusalem has the temple of God. Babylon's origins are based on the confusion and division found at the Tower of Babel; Jerusalem's origins are based on God's clear and eternal covenant with Abraham. Babylon is a center of sin; Jerusalem is set apart to holiness. Babylon is destined to destruction; Jerusalem is to be the eternal Holy City.

If Jerusalem is the city of God, then, as the antithesis, Babylon is the city of Satan. What we see in chapters 17 and 18 are a foreshadow of the final destruction of the devil and his ways.

First, in chapter 17, we witness the fall of the world religious system that had controlled the global political and economic structures. The woman sitting on the beast had led the masses into religious idolatry. But her hold on the hearts of the people will collapse under the domination of the world powers.

Then, in chapter 18, God destroys the political and economic system in the brief span of sixty minutes: "Alas, alas, that great city Babylon, that mighty city! For in one hour your judgment has come" (Revelation 18:10). Remember the collapse of the American economy at the beginning of the coronavirus? In a very short time, the US went from having one of the best economies in the nation's history to mass unemployment, a plunging stock market, and businesses shutting down all over the country. That is nothing compared to what awaits the global economy in Revelation 18. It will make the stock market collapse of 1929 and the ensuing Great Depression look like child's play.

REVELATION 19:
A WONDERFUL WEDDING

From Revelation 4 until now, we have followed the narrative of the discipline of Israel and the punishment of unbelievers. In chapter 19, the church steps back into the story, and when it returns, it does so in beauty and strength.

John's narrative leaves the earth and moves back to events in heaven. What he heard when he got there was a lot of hallelujahing going on.

Hallelujah means "God be praised" or "Praise the Lord." It is a shout of thanksgiving and praise and affirmation and awe and wow. John heard this joyous exclamation first from a great multitude (19:1,3), then from the twenty-four elders and the four creatures (verse 4), and then again from a great multitude (verse 6). All were praising the Lord, calling out His greatness. What is all this celebration about? The destruction of the prostitute of Satan, Babylon, and the marriage of the bride of Christ, the church.

We don't know what this heavenly marriage ceremony of Christ to His bride will look like. Every culture has its own traditions for marriage, and most of them are very emotional and beautiful. It's likely that what we as the church will experience in our union with our Savior will be unlike anything we can think or imagine. Love beyond comprehension; beauty beyond measure.

Celebrating this union, the voice of the multitude cried out, "Alleluia! For the Lord God Omnipotent reigns! Let us be glad and rejoice and give Him glory, for the marriage of the Lamb has come, and His wife has made herself ready" (verses 6-7). John then described the bride: "To her it was granted to be arrayed in fine linen, clean and bright, for the fine linen is the righteous acts of the saints" (verse 8). The bride, coming forth from the ceremony, was now ready for the great marriage feast.

It had to be a surreal experience for John to see the bride, knowing that he himself was somewhere in that mass of people. Did he catch a glimpse of himself sporting his new resurrection body? Did he and future John lock eyes, with his future self smiling knowingly at him?

John's encounter with the bride was overwhelming. At one point he became so emotional at what he was witnessing that he fell down in worship of the angel who was with him. The angel was quick to stop him. "See that you do not do that! I am your fellow servant, and of your brethren who have the testimony of Jesus. Worship God! For the testimony of Jesus is the spirit of prophecy" (verse 10). There are great men and women on this earth. There are powerful spiritual beings all around us. But there is no one and nothing that is worthy of our worship other than God our Father and His Son, Jesus Christ.

Now that we've met the bride, it's time to introduce the groom:

> Now I saw heaven opened, and behold, a white horse. And He who sat on him was called Faithful and True, and in righteousness He judges and makes war. His eyes were like a flame of fire, and on His head were many crowns. He had a name written that no one knew except Himself. He was clothed with a robe dipped in blood, and His name is called The Word of God. And the armies in heaven, clothed in fine linen, white and clean, followed Him on white horses. Now out of His mouth goes a sharp sword, that with it He should strike the nations. And He Himself will rule them with a rod of iron. He Himself treads the winepress of the fierceness and wrath of Almighty God. And He has on His robe and on His thigh a name written:
>
> KING OF KINGS AND
> LORD OF LORDS (verses 11-16).

This is awe-inspiring! Jesus Christ, in all His glory, will return to earth at the second coming. And we will return with Him, gathered behind Him and ready for battle. I've often said that when Jesus first returns, we will want to see His front. We will see Him face to face as He gathers us in the clouds at the rapture. At the second coming, we will want to see His back. If we see Him from behind, that means that we are following Him as He goes forth to battle. If we see Him from the front at the second coming, then we are the ones He is coming to do battle with, and we had better run!

There is never a doubt as to the outcome of the great battle. How do you beat an all-powerful foe? You don't. Jesus will have the victory. The enemy forces will be obliterated, and the beast and the false prophet will be the first to be cast into the lake of fire.

At this time, the church will be back on the earth, with everyone in their new resurrected bodies. Who else will remain in the world? There will be the tribulation saints who somehow managed to survive to the end without getting martyred. And there will be the Jews—God's people, whom He has spared until now. This is the great moment that I long to witness—the moment Paul speaks of in Romans when he writes, "All Israel will be saved, as it is written: 'The Deliverer will come out of Zion, and He will turn away ungodliness from Jacob; for this is My covenant with them, when I take away their sins'" (Romans 11:26-27). This mass revival will take place as the Jews finally recognize the Messiah, whom they had rejected, for who He truly is. Every man and woman and child will willingly surrender themselves to Jesus Christ, making Him both their Savior and their Lord. What a glorious day that will be!

REVELATION 20: PLANET EARTH UNDER NEW MANAGEMENT

With Christ back on earth, the world will be under new management. Until this point, Satan had authority over this planet. Jesus called him "the ruler of this world" (John 12:31) and Paul referred to him as "the god of this world" (2 Corinthians 4:4 ESV). But the devil's time on this earth is done—mostly. John watched as an angel approached Satan:

> He laid hold of the dragon, that serpent of old, who is the Devil and Satan, and bound him for a thousand years; and he cast him into the bottomless pit, and shut him up, and set a seal on him, so that he should deceive the nations no more till the thousand years were finished. But after these things he must be released for a little while (Revelation 20:2-3).

This begins the millennial kingdom. For 1,000 years, Christ will reign from Jerusalem. It will be a time of peace and righteousness. But the righteousness will not last. Even though Satan is not around, there will be people who still live in bodies of flesh. Even if the devil isn't around to "make one do it," there will be people who have the sin-nature-propensity to go ahead and do it anyway. That's why, when Satan is released back into the world after his millennium in captivity, he will find a ready audience in the strayed progeny of those Jews and surviving tribulation saints who entered the millennial kingdom in their mortal bodies.

Satan will organize a rebellion that will manifest itself in a second battle of Gog and Magog. Again, the defeat of the rebels will be swift and certain. All who are against God will be wiped out, and the devil will be cast into the lake of fire to join the beast and the false prophet. Right now Satan thinks he has power, but the only power he has is that which God grants him. When his time is done, he will be done.

Revelation 20 ends with the Great White Throne judgment, which we will look at in the next chapter of this book.

REVELATION 21:
BACK TO THE DRAWING BOARD

When sin entered the world, death came with it. This included spiritual death, which resulted in mankind's separation from a holy God, and physical death, which led to a deterioration of all of creation. In Revelation 21, because the old heaven and earth are defiled beyond being salvable, God will go back to the drawing board and create a new heaven and a new earth, then the new Jerusalem will descend from the sky.

"Behold, I make all things new" (Revelation 21:5), the Lord will say from His throne. We are not given a glimpse at what Heaven and Earth 2.0 will look like. However, if they are anything like New Jerusalem, then they will be beyond spectacular. Of the upgraded Holy City, John writes:

> The construction of its wall was of jasper; and the city was pure gold, like clear glass. The foundations of the wall of the city were adorned with all kinds of precious stones: the first foundation was jasper, the second sapphire, the third chalcedony, the fourth emerald, the fifth sardonyx, the sixth sardius, the seventh chrysolite, the eighth beryl, the ninth topaz, the tenth chrysoprase, the eleventh jacinth, and the twelfth amethyst. The twelve gates were twelve pearls: each individual gate was of one pearl. And the street

of the city was pure gold, like transparent glass. But I saw no temple in it, for the Lord God Almighty and the Lamb are its temple. The city had no need of the sun or of the moon to shine in it, for the glory of God illuminated it. The Lamb is its light (verses 18-23).

How John's elderly eyes must have sparkled, reflecting the jewels as they shone with the light of Christ. We may not know what the new heaven and earth will look like, but we can be sure of one thing—we will not be disappointed.

REVELATION 22:
READY OR NOT, HERE I COME

This last chapter of Revelation looks back on the Lord's promise to return for His own. In a way, the last chapter brings us back to our time—to our reality—and it speaks of the love of God, the hope for the believer, the wages of sin, which is death, and, of course, the free gift of eternal life. It speaks of prophecy revealed in the book and the urgency of our task as Christ's ambassadors. Jesus said, "Behold, I am coming quickly! Blessed is he who keeps the words of the prophecy of this book" (Revelation 22:7).

Jesus was speaking these words to the churches of the first century, but He is also talking to us. We are the bride, and the Spirit is in us. We need to eagerly wait for His coming to take us to be with Him. "The Spirit and the bride say, 'Come!' And let him who hears say, 'Come!' And let him who thirsts come. Whoever desires, let him take the water of life freely" (verse 17). We need to join this chorus with our cries for Jesus to come soon.

By the way, just because you want Jesus to come does not mean you have been defeated by the world. This desire for Christ's return is an attitude we should have all the time. I remember when I was very depressed during my first few weeks in the military. I didn't want to stay there a minute longer. It was very hard, very tough. Every night during my guard shift, I would ask Jesus to come back. "Really, Lord— any minute now. I'm ready!" For me, thinking of Christ's return was comforting. There was a song I used to sing: "Ana hazor na Yeshua, Melech HaYehudim," or "Please come back, Yeshua, the King of the Jews." My plea was truly from the heart. "I am ready anytime You're ready, Lord Jesus!"

The promise of what is to come should be a great encouragement to all of us in the church.

Sin must be punished, but God's grace is great. No one on this earth has to suffer the terrors described in Revelation. Sadly, there are so very many who will choose to endure the tribulation by rejecting Jesus' free offer of salvation through faith in Him. For those of us in the church, this biblical book should serve as an impetus to be about our Father's business until we are taken to the grave or to the clouds.

The promise of what is to come should be a great encouragement to all of us in the church. Paul wrote to the Thessalonians, "God did not appoint us to wrath, but to obtain salvation through our Lord Jesus Christ, who died for us, that whether we wake or sleep, we should live together with Him. Therefore comfort each other and edify one another, just as you also are doing" (1 Thessalonians 5:9-11). We will not be here for the judgments poured out during the tribulation. We will be with our Savior. To be in His presence and see His face should be motivation enough for us to echo the words of the elderly apostle, writer, and friend of the Savior: "Even so, come, Lord Jesus!" (verse 20).

PART 4:

TWO PEOPLES, ONE FAMILY

CHAPTER 11

WHO GOES WHERE?

*A Place for Everyone
and Everyone in Their Place*

Who goes where?

This is a question that most people ask at some point in their lives. When we die, where do we go? Do some go up and others go down? Do we end up cycling around again for another shot at life—hopefully doing a little better the next time? Do we all end up in the same place—that is, do all religious roads lead to heaven? Is there a different plan of salvation for the Jews than there is for the church—one for the people of the old covenant, and one for the new? How does all this work?

Most of the time, people try to avoid questions about death. In fact, they prefer to not think about dying at all. It's an uncomfortable subject—even a little scary. But there are times when we are all confronted with what happens after death. This is particularly true at funerals. Often you will hear people talking about their loved ones looking down on them from heaven or walking next to them and protecting them, or becoming one of God's newest angels. We can't fault them for grasping hold of such hopes in their struggles to deal with grief. Sadly, though, they are just feel-good ideas that have no theological backing.

Few questions are more important than those about the afterlife because death, for all of us, is essentially right around the corner. Where do we go when we die? Some are asking this question because they've lost their parents. Some are asking about what will happen to nonbelievers they know. Some are curious about what happened to Old Testament people compared to those they read about in the New Testament. There are even those who are desperate to know where their dearly departed pets are. If this last one includes you, I need to let you know up front that this book will not give you the answer as to where your emotional support pony is dwelling now that it's eaten its last sugar cube.

What is next for us once this life is over? And what about all those who have gone before?

ALL WAS GOOD—UNTIL THE FALL

God made the earth to be a wonderful place for mankind to dwell. Heaven wasn't initially made for people. Terra firma was our intended abode. From the hair on our heads to the calluses on our feet, we were programmed, planned, and designed to spend our time on this third planet from the sun.

And what a place God gave to us! Initially it was perfect in every way. On the first day, after creating the light, "God saw the light, that it was good" (Genesis 1:4). With every successive act of creation, that same adjective of perfection was declared. Land—good. Seas—good. Vegetation—good. Everything was created in its optimal state.

At the earth's founding, nobody was afraid of a tornado or a hurricane or a flood. There were no flus or coronaviruses or cancers. No financial collapses were on the horizon and no one was afraid of war suddenly breaking out. Adam and Eve had been given a marvelous place and were told to enjoy it.

The earth was given to those first two humans not only to live on, but to have dominion over. If the lions were getting too rowdy, Adam would simply need to say, "Hey, lions, come over here. Now sit down. I want you to behave and quit scaring all the rabbits." The lions would obey, and the rabbits would breathe a sigh of relief.

But the best part for Adam and Eve was that God dwelled with them. He would descend from on high to fellowship with mankind. Can you imagine? After a long day of work, God would leave His throne to go strolling in the Garden. The first couple enjoyed perfect fellowship with the Creator. But then Adam and Eve decided this was not enough. Someone else came along with a new message that was more exciting. The serpent spun a lie, and they quite literally bit. They broke the trust, the fellowship, that which made them the crown jewel of creation—the image of God inside of them.

What a disappointment. That first sin set mankind on a course that took us further and further away from God. Like an avalanche sliding down a mountainside, the devastation and destruction grew with every successive generation. Finally, after many years had passed, "the LORD saw that the wickedness of man was great in the earth, and that every intent of the thoughts of his heart was only evil continually. And the LORD was sorry that He had made man on the earth, and He was grieved in His heart" (Genesis 6:5-6). God provided one opportunity after another for people to hear His warnings and make their hearts right—a flood, fire and brimstone raining down, a new nation chosen to be a living testimony of Him. But nothing could get through the sin-scarred hearts of mankind.

GOD'S LOVE REACHES OUT

But then something changed. Two thousand years ago, God sent His Son to redeem us sinners—all of us rebels who had turned our backs on Him: God reached out to us. If I were God, I wouldn't have done that. I probably would have scoured the fine print in the contract trying to find an out-clause to the whole "no more worldwide flood" covenant. It's a good thing I'm not God.

Rather than attack, God sacrificed. He did it because He is love. He loves with a never-ending kind of love. People disappoint Him, but He keeps loving them. People hate Him, but He keeps loving them. People betray Him, but He never stops loving them.

God's love led Him to send His only Son to die on the cross for our forgiveness and redemption from our deserved judgment. Then He sent the Holy Spirit to fill and seal us, marking us as His own and giving birth to the church. And one day the Father is going to send His Son again to take us from this earth to be with Him in heaven. This will restore that one-on-one fellowship that was lost so long ago in the Garden.

Imagine that day when we will be taken from this earth to meet our Savior in the air. We'll briefly congregate with Him and all the believers from the church age. Then we will ascend to the place that He has spent 2,000 years preparing for us. We have no idea what it is going to look like, but we can be certain we will be amazed and overwhelmed.

After this comes the only move in this whole wonderful plan that I wonder about. Seven years after taking us up to be with Him, the Father is going to send His Son—along with all of us in the church—back down to earth. Why do we have to come back? Jesus has been working on my mansion for two millennia, and as soon as I get the boxes unpacked from my move, I've got to come back down here? Oy, Lord, couldn't You give us a couple hundred years to enjoy our new home before we leave it all behind for a while?

But God has a reason for us to return. There is still more of His plan He wants to accomplish through His church. This is also the time when all Israel will be saved. This isn't a result of God saying, "Hey, you're My people, we're going to ignore all those sins you committed in the past. No biggie—everybody makes mistakes." Remember, Jesus said, "I am the way, the truth, and the life. No one comes to the Father except through Me" (John 14:6). Those words "no one" include every person from all times past and future. Sins can only be removed through Christ's blood. He is the only way to reconciliation with God.

When we in the church are back on this earth, we will reign with Christ for 1,000 years. Then God will bring final judgment on the world—a time that is gut-wrenching just to think about. When sin has been dealt with once and for all, He will fashion the new heavens and a new earth, and will bring the New Jerusalem down from the sky.

DEATH IS NOT THE END

I give you this timeline to emphasize that when you die—if you die—it is not the end. There is so much more that the Bible promises for the future. And if you have a relationship with Christ, all that future is good and all of it involves God. His plan has always been for fellowship with us, and eternity is all about spending time with our Creator.

There are those who say that the idea of an afterlife in God's presence isn't found early in Judaism. They say the concept was added at a later point in the development of the Jews' belief system. But that is not true. The book of Job is oldest in the Bible. It is estimated that its author picked up his pen way back in the time of the patriarchs—somewhere between 1900–1700 BC. Even that early in our historical timeline, the suffering protagonist of the story anticipated he would one day see God face to face:

> For I know that my Redeemer lives,
> And He shall stand at last on the earth;
> And after my skin is destroyed, this I know,
> That in my flesh I shall see God,
> Whom I shall see for myself,
> And my eyes shall behold, and not another.
> How my heart yearns within me (Job 19:25-27).

Job longed for the day when he would meet his Redeemer in person. He didn't say, "Look, one day I will spiritually experience my Redeemer's powerful presence surrounding me." Or, "Allegorically, I will behold Him as representative of some greater truth." Rather, he said, "My Redeemer lives…whom I shall see for myself." He didn't say he was going to see some representation of God or some parabolic vision. He wouldn't have to settle for watching God on closed-circuit television. One day in the flesh, his eyes will behold his Redeemer. When I think of that day, I, too, feel my heart yearning along with Job's.

While the afterlife sounds wonderful for believers, for unbelievers, the future is not nearly so rosy. For believers it's all about fellowship; for unbelievers it's all about punishment. When I was in the military, when we were in the mood to break a few rules, we would normally do so on the weekend. Our thinking was that because it was Shabbat, the commanders would be busy and we had a better chance of getting away with what we had planned. But one of my commanders would always remind us, "There is an evening when Shabbat is over." In other words, you can have your fun now, but know that eventually the punishment will come. It was his way of telling us that if we were going to do the crime, then we better be prepared to do the time.

There was one Shabbat evening when doing the time involved performing a funeral for a little piece of cigarette. The commander had come by to inspect our barracks, and there in the middle of the floor was a fragment of someone's cigarette. That was all it took to prove to him that rather than cleaning our living quarters as we had been told to do, instead, we had done our own thing. He made us gently lift that little cigarette butt off the floor and place it carefully onto a stretcher. We then carried it out the door and proceeded to march it around in the middle of the desert for two hours. Then that tiny bit of paper, filter, and tobacco received a full-blown memorial service followed by a proper burial. And just to make sure his point had been made, the commander continued our memorial march until Saturday p.m. became Sunday a.m. When the sun rose and we again stepped in time past the little mound of dirt that marked the burial spot of our tiny deceased companion, I gained a special understanding of the passage about Mary coming to the tomb early Sunday morning (see John 20:1).

Most people are going through life playing like it's Shabbat day and the commander is at home with his family, ignoring the fact that sundown is coming soon. Hebrews 9:27 says, "It is appointed for men to die once, but after this the judgment." In other words, if you're thinking that once you're dead it's all over, it isn't. After this life, it's judgment time. When Hannah gave celebratory praise after God blessed her with a son, she prayed, "The LORD kills and makes alive; He brings down to the grave and brings up" (1 Samuel 2:6). When your body is laid in the grave, that's not the end. God brings down every life, and He will bring back up every life.

THE FUTURE PLAN FOR ISRAEL

There is a future for believers and unbelievers—a conscious eternity where we will either enjoy the rewards or suffer the consequences for the decisions we make in this life. There is a third group of people that God has created a distinct future for, and that is the nation of Israel. In Daniel 12, the prophet's angelic visitor spoke to him, saying, "At that time Michael shall stand up, the great prince who stands watch over the sons of your people" (Daniel 12:1). "Your people" is clearly speaking of Israel. This is evident by the identification two chapters earlier that Michael is the archangel who serves as the prince of Israel.

---

*Eternity is for everyone—believers and unbelievers,
Jews and Gentiles. And like in real estate, the most
important factor is location, location, location.*

A Time of Trouble Is Coming

The message that was brought to Daniel was not one of good news: "There shall be a time of trouble, such as never was since there was a nation" (Daniel 12:1). This time of trouble is those seven years of misery and sorrow that we've been talking about known as the tribulation. It is that period of suffering that will ultimately lead to Israel's salvation.

The angel continued,

> At that time your people shall be delivered, every one who is found written in the book. And many of those who sleep in the dust of the earth shall awake, some to everlasting life, some to shame and everlasting contempt. Those who are wise shall shine like the brightness of the firmament, and those who turn many to righteousness like the stars forever and ever (Daniel 12:1-3).

There is a future for Israel. God is not done with the Jewish people. There will be an attempt to destroy them that will surpass all previous attempts, some of which have been significant. But, through the mercy of God, the nation will survive and will pass into the millennial kingdom. Some of the Jews entering that 1,000-year reign of Jesus will be part of the mass revival within the nation at the end of the tribulation. Some will be those sleeping "in the dust of the earth [who] shall awake" (verse 2).

Eternity is for everyone—believers and unbelievers, Jews and Gentiles. And like in real estate, the most important factor is location, location, location.

The Resurrection Is Coming

One day a group of Sadducees came to test Jesus. The Sadducees were of the priestly families and were therefore the cream of Israel's socioeconomic hierarchy. Unlike the Pharisees, who truly hated Jesus and all that He stood for, these guys just thought that Jesus was beneath them. To them, He was some country rube from the backwater town of Nazareth. They probably figured they could quickly and easily put this bumpkin in His proper place and still make it to the country club in time for a late champagne brunch. So they gathered together and concocted a story that they were sure would trip up Jesus and make Him look like the fool they believed Him to be.

The tactic the Sadducees decided to use was to ask a question about the resurrection. This was the key theological issue that set them apart from the Pharisees. The Sadducees didn't believe in life after death; the Pharisees did. Isn't it interesting that in this case Jesus ends up siding with the Pharisees, the ones who had taken an oath to kill him?

This group of Sadducees said to Jesus, "Teacher, Moses wrote to us that if a man's brother dies, having a wife, and he dies without children, his brother should take his wife and raise up offspring for his brother" (Luke 20:28). They started out with the law. Brilliant tactic. "You do agree with the law, don't you, Rabbi?" What else could Jesus say but yes? In their minds, Jesus would be forced to step into their noose, then they would yank it tight.

They continued, "Now there were seven brothers. And the first took a wife, and died without children. And the second took her as wife, and he died childless. Then the third took her, and in like manner the seven also; and they left no children, and died. Last of all the woman died also. Therefore, in the resurrection, whose wife does she become? For all seven had her as wife" (Luke 20:29-33). Boom! Game, set, match! Drop the mic and walk offstage! In a scenario that sounds like a poly-andric plot twist to an old musical, *Seven Brides for Seven Brothers*, the Sadducees had laid out a theological and marital Gordian knot. You can almost picture them smugly leaning back and crossing their arms with haughty and condescending looks on their faces.

Jesus' response is beautiful. "You are mistaken, not knowing the Scriptures nor the power of God" (Matthew 22:29). Can you imag-ine the change to their faces when this upstart Galilean carpenter told them that not only do they not know their Bibles, but they have no clue how God works? Him—telling them! I would have loved to have been a fly on the Temple wall, watching this dialogue unfold.

But Jesus wasn't content to stop with the insult. He was brash enough to attempt to set them straight. "The sons of this age marry and are given in marriage. But those who are counted worthy to attain that age, and the resurrection from the dead, neither marry nor are given in marriage; nor can they die anymore, for they are equal to the angels and are sons of God, being sons of the resurrection" (Luke 20:34-36). "Only those who are counted worthy," He said, implying that maybe because the Saddu-cees don't believe in the afterlife, they won't be there for the resurrection. "Sorry, Sadducees, you aren't quite elite enough to be invited to this party."

Jesus was telling them they had it all wrong. There truly is some thing after this life is over. He was saying, "Guys, do you think that after your marriage here on earth, God would punish you with mar-riage in heaven?"

(Wait! Pick the book back up—that's just a joke!)

Jesus told them that the way life is here and the way life will be in heaven are very different. On the other side of death, we will not be hubby hubby and wifey wifey. The sons and daughters of the resurrec-tion will be much more reminiscent of angels. Heaven will not be a place of marriage and interpersonal struggles and sexual tension.

This sets us apart from so many other faiths. Young Muslim men are told, "Blow yourself up, and you'll have seventy-two virgins." What a promise—how spiritual! Their emphasis is not on holiness; it's not on God. It's on that same lust of the flesh that causes so many problems already here on earth. The lust of the eyes, the lust of the flesh, and the sinful pride of life are not going to be imported into the perfection of heaven.

Jesus drove the final nail in the Sadducees' coffin when He concluded, "Even Moses showed in the burning bush passage that the dead are raised, when he called the Lord 'the God of Abraham, the God of Isaac, and the God of Jacob.' For He is not the God of the dead but of the living, for all live to Him" (Luke 20:37-38). If they really wanted to worship the god of the dead, they could bow down to the false god Hades. But if they want to worship the true God—the God of the living—then they must worship the God of Abraham, Isaac, and Jacob. And if He is the God of the living, then Abraham and Isaac and Jacob must be alive somewhere. Who knows? If you get your beliefs right, you Sadducees, you just might end up meeting them someday.

Throughout His ministry, Jesus made it clear that there is more to life than just our time on this earth. Which brings us back to our original question: When death comes, what happens next? Who goes where? An old adage says, "A place for everything, and everything in its place." Our God loves order. He has ordered history and He has ordered the future. He has ordered the seasons and He has ordered our days. He has ordered heaven, He has ordered hell, and He has formulated a plan for determining who, ultimately, will inhabit each.

GOD MAKES THE PLANS

In the order that God has laid out, there are several time periods. This includes the time of the Old Testament and the time of the New Testament. He also spells out the church age, the tribulation, and the millennial kingdom. How do I know about these time periods? From the Bible. The Bible shows when the Old Testament ended. The Bible tells us how many years passed until God spoke again. The Bible demonstrates in its final words that the New Testament is complete. The church age, tribulation, and the millennium are all directly from the pages of the Word of God.

This flow of the future didn't originate in Amir's Imagination Workshop. I wasn't sitting out on my porch one day looking out over the Valley of Megiddo when I was suddenly hit with the thought, *Wouldn't it be great if something really big happened out there in those fertile tracts of farmland? I don't know—maybe a big battle of some kind. It could be at the end of a really trying time—an adversity of sorts. No, more than adversity—a real tribulation. Once that's over with, maybe it could lead to a really long period of good times. A hundred years? No, too short. Five hundred? Almost, but not quite. A thousand years! That's it—one thousand years of good times—so good that even lions will want to lie down with lambs.* There is no book of Amir in the Bible. I am not a prophet. I'd never want to be a prophet. I don't like the taste of locusts and I don't look good in camel hair. All these time periods I've mentioned are directly from the Word of God. That's why we never have to guess or wonder or doubt.

The First and Second Births

If we're going to talk about what happens after we die, we first need to discuss birth. Without birth, there is no death. In the Bible, we find two types of birth. The first birth is from the water. We all start out as great swimmers. This is because for nine months we are treading water in our mother's womb. Then the water breaks and the pool is emptied. Once the water is gone, it's our indication that it's time to relocate. So out we come.

Now if you think that this new sweet bundle of joy is sinless and pure as the wind-driven snow, you can kiss that thought goodbye. David said, "Behold, I was brought forth in iniquity, and in sin my mother conceived me" (Psalm 51:5). From the beginning, we were steeped in sin. In Romans, Paul said, "Just as through one man sin entered the world, and death through sin, and thus death spread to all men, because all sinned" (5:12; cf. Genesis 6:5; Ephesians 2:1-3). Adam's sin put a taint in humanity that is carried from generation to generation.

We are not born as saints, and we spend our lives demonstrating our lack of sainthood.

When I take people to Nazareth on my tours, we often go to a shopping area where we are given a view of where the old town used to be. Across a valley, we can see the topography of Jesus' childhood. Today the entire hillside is built up with houses and shopping areas and churches, but with some imagination, we can still picture the young boy running and playing. With our mind's eye, we can see the teenager walking the dusty streets with his friends and assisting His earthly father in his carpentry business.

While we're all gathered on that viewing balcony, I always set aside time to also teach the group about what happened in that town one night. We talk about a late meeting that Jesus had with a certain Pharisee who came to Him. I tell them, "Do you know that not one of you was born born again? In fact, nobody has ever been born born again. In order to be born again, you must first be born. Then once you are born, you can become born again."

My point is that there is a first birth, and it is with sin. Because of this inherited sin nature, we are by nature children of wrath. Jesus told Nicodemus, His nighttime visitor,

> God so loved the world that He gave His only begotten Son, that whoever believes in Him should not perish but have everlasting life. For God did not send His Son into the world to condemn the world, but that the world through Him might be saved. He who believes in Him is not condemned; but he who does not believe is condemned already, because he has not believed in the name of the only begotten Son of God (John 3:16-18).

Notice the words "condemned already." Every one of us was, at one time, in that category. We were all conducting ourselves according to the desires of our flesh. But even without our later sins, we would still have been in the "condemned already" camp because we had been born there. It is only through faith in Jesus that we are brought out of "condemned already" and into "not condemned."

That first birth is the birth of the flesh. The second birth, however, is from the Spirit. When sin is forgiven and taken away, something astounding happens. Jesus said, "Most assuredly, I say to you, he who hears My word and believes in Him who sent Me has everlasting life, and shall not come into judgment, but has passed from death into life" (John 5:24). Your decision to believe in God and trust Jesus for your salvation completely changes your story. Where once there was only death in your future, now there is life.

When Jesus spent time with the Samaritan woman, He said to her, "Woman, believe Me, the hour is coming when you will neither on this mountain, nor in Jerusalem, worship the Father. You worship what you do not know; we know what we worship, for salvation is of the Jews. But the hour is coming, and now is, when the true worshipers will worship the Father in spirit and truth; for the Father is seeking such to worship Him" (John 4:21-23). Jesus was telling her that the rules to the game have changed. It is no longer about where you worship, but how you worship. It doesn't matter if it is at the Temple; it may not be in Jerusalem at all. Under the new rules, you don't have to go anywhere to be a true worshipper as long as you are worshipping Him in spirit and in truth—with our hearts and with our minds.

When we were born of our mother's wombs—born of water only we came into the world condemned already. Then came the second birth from the Spirit and we were made new. "If anyone is in Christ, he is a new creation; old things have passed away; behold, all things have become new" (2 Corinthians 5:17; cf. Titus 3:4-5). No wonder Jesus told Nicodemus, "You must be born again" (John 3:7). Not *should*, but *must*. It's the new birth that makes all the difference.

The First and Second Deaths

There is a first birth and there is a second birth. Similarly, there is a first death and a second death. The first death is one we all will experience—all except for those believers who will still be alive on earth at the time of the rapture. This first death is the natural consequence of sin. You may be thinking, *What do you mean I'm going to die? Paul said*

I've passed from death to life. That's true, you have been made spiritually new. But you are still in this original body of yours—you are new inside, but with the same old packaging. The corruptible body is just that—corruptible—and is subject to diseases and deterioration. The Bible refers to it as your "lowly body" (Philippians 3:21).

"But, Amir, I eat right and I work out every day." Great, so you'll die healthy. You'll be a beautiful corpse. You can work out to your heart's content, then leave the gym and get run down by a car in the parking lot. The natural consequence of sin is the first death, and it's coming for all of us.

For the unbeliever, this first death is something to be greatly feared. Jesus said, "Do not fear those who kill the body but cannot kill the soul. But rather fear Him who is able to destroy both soul and body in hell" (Matthew 10:28). If you don't believe in Jesus as your Savior and Lord, then death should terrify you. There is a God, and there is a judgment coming. You may act as if neither exists, but that doesn't change the fact that they do exist and that you will be held accountable one day for your life on this earth.

———————————

Every person...will experience resurrection. The only differences between them will be in the timing of their resurrection and what they will be resurrected to.

———————————

Jesus told the story of a rich man and a poor man. The rich man lived his life enjoying his wealth, caring about nobody but himself. The poor man, Lazarus, suffered every day of his sojourn on this earth. Lazarus died "and was carried by the angels to Abraham's bosom. The rich man also died and was buried. And being in torments in Hades, he lifted up his eyes and saw Abraham afar off, and Lazarus in his bosom" (Luke 16:22-23). Both men died and both went to Hades. However, there was a separation in Hades between the place of torment and

Abraham's bosom. They could see each other, but they couldn't get to each other—not that Lazarus would have wanted to try. He was on the good side, the believing side—the place of peace and safety and comfort. The rich man was across the divide on the unbelieving side—the place of sorrow and regret and suffering.

It's a revelation to many to learn that prior to Jesus' death, the believer and unbeliever both went to Hades. That can be a hard concept to grasp because we tend to associate Hades with hell. But they are two different places. Hell is the lake of fire—a place of eternal punishment—which doesn't come into play until the final judgment at the end of time. Hades, however, is a temporary holding place. Picture the waiting room for your doctor, minus the fake plants and the magazines from 2014. It's not your final destination—it's just the place where you mark time until the door opens and your name is called. We don't know where this post-death waiting room is. Is it up above, or is it down below? Is it a physical place, or is it a spiritual dwelling? The only clues we get from Jesus' story have to do with the structural layout and the physical and emotional states of the inhabitants.

What will happen when the door to the waiting room is opened? Resurrection. Every person, no matter which side of the room they're waiting in, will experience resurrection. The only differences between them will be in the timing of their resurrection and what they will be resurrected to.

It's important to note that what is not behind the door is a second chance. There is no postmortem second chance at salvation. This is also not purgatory. You're not going to work your way out of your final destination by being tormented for a couple thousand years. Your chance for salvation dies when you die.

Before the cross, all took the same road to Hades, but got off at different exits. After the cross, the believer's destination changed. When Jesus was suffering and near death, one of the thieves hanging on a cross next to Him said, "'Lord, remember me when You come into Your kingdom.' And Jesus said to him, 'Assuredly, I say to you, today you will be with Me in Paradise'" (Luke 23:42-43). These words were a game-changer. Before the cross, when the faithful were made absent from the body, they became present at Abraham's bosom. Now we know that "to be absent from the body [is] to be present with the Lord" (2 Corinthians 5:8). Instantly. Eyes close here, eyes open there, and you see Jesus' face.

TWO KINDS OF PEOPLE, TWO DESTINIES

Ultimately there are two kinds of people: believers and unbelievers. There are also two categories of believers: those before the cross and those after. Each has gone or will go to a different temporary destination when they die. Unbelievers from all time go to the torment side of Hades; Old Testament believers went to the happy side of Hades; and church-age believers enter the presence of the Lord.

Most of us will die—maybe sooner, maybe later—but there are some of us who won't because we will be raptured. If you're a believer in Jesus, both of those options are great. Paul encouraged the Corinthians with these words: "We are always confident, knowing that while we are at home in the body we are absent from the Lord. For we walk by faith, not by sight. We are confident, yes, well pleased rather to be absent from the body and to be present with the Lord" (2 Corinthians 5:6-8). Death no longer holds a sting for us.

"I understand that, Amir, but I still don't want to die." Okay, then don't. I'd recommend heavy doses of Vitamin C and maybe wrapping your home with bubble wrap. But if death does find you one day and you have Jesus as your Savior, then go boldly into that dark night knowing that the glory of God's light is right around the corner.

Praise the Lord, we have no bad options. This magnificent truth caused a personal struggle within Paul. He wrote, "For to me, to live is Christ, and to die is gain. But if I live on in the flesh, this will mean fruit from my labor; yet what I shall choose I cannot tell. For I am hard-pressed between the two, having a desire to depart and be with Christ, which is far better" (Philippians 1:21-23). That's the glorious life of the believer. I'm hard-pressed between life and death. I really want to go to be with my Savior. But since He's still got me here for now, I'll spend the time I have left living for Him.

Thus far, we've only dealt with the first death. There is also a second death. The first death is the physical consequence of sin. The second death is sin's spiritual consequence. What is death? It is a disconnection from the source of life. Where there is no life, there is death.

Physically, we start with life, then move toward death. Spiritually, however, we are born dead. Even though our bodies are animated and we have full function of our faculties, inside we are "dead in trespasses and sins" (Ephesians 2:1). Spiritual death is eternal. We are born spiritually dead, we live spiritually dead, and when our physical life ends, our spiritual death carries on into eternity. As with physical death, sin is the cause of our spiritual death. It is what separates us from God, who is the source of life. Therefore, if we still carry our sins, we have no life because we are not connected to its source.

That's where the good news comes in. Physically, we will only move from life toward death. Spiritually, through Jesus Christ, the door opens for us to move from death to life. The Savior said, "Most assuredly, I say to you, he who hears My word and believes in Him who sent Me has everlasting life, and shall not come into judgment, but has passed from death into life" (John 5:24). The death He spoke of here is the second death. There is no more judgment in store for us; we become part of the "not condemned." As the prodigal's father said, "It was right that we should make merry and be glad, for your brother was dead and is alive again, and was lost and is found" (Luke 15:32).

It is only through Christ that we can be spared from the second death. He is the only one with the power and authority to hold command over death and Hades. Jesus said, "I am He who lives, and was dead, and behold, I am alive forevermore. Amen. And I have the keys of Hades and of Death" (Revelation 1:18). At the final judgment, Jesus will put those keys to use. "The sea gave up the dead who were in it, and Death and Hades delivered up the dead who were in them. And they were judged, each one according to his works. Then Death and Hades were cast into the lake of fire. This is the second death" (Revelation 20:13-14). Jesus will open the doors of Death and Hades, resurrect those who are being kept there awaiting final judgment, then send each person to their final destination.

And, yes, I did say that He will even resurrect those in Hades. Just as there are two births and two deaths, there are two resurrections. When Jesus rose from the grave, He started something new. He was the first person to live, die, live again, and never die again. Lazarus, the widow's son, and all the others who returned from the dead eventually died again. Only Jesus never returned to the grave. Thus, He was the first-fruits of the first resurrection.

In time, others will follow. The next resurrection will take place at the rapture and will deliver new incorruptible bodies to the church-age saints (John 14:1-4), followed immediately by those believers who are still alive on earth at the time (1 Corinthians 15:50-54; 1 Thessalonians 4:15-18). During the tribulation, in what is sure to be quite the media spectacle, the two witnesses will be resurrected (Revelation 11:11-12). Then at the second coming of Christ, the Old Testament saints (Daniel 12:1-2,13; Isaiah 26:19) and the tribulation martyrs (Revelation 20:4-6) will put on their new upgraded flesh. All these are part of the blessed first resurrection.

Finally, at the end of time, will come the second resurrection. Just like the second death, this is not one you want to be part of. "I saw a great white throne and Him who sat on it, from whose face the earth and the heaven fled away. And there was found no place for them. And I saw the dead, small and great, standing before God, and books were opened" (Revelation 20:11-12). In heaven, there is a stack of books. These are the books of life, and they contain a list of everyone who has ever been born. When you enter the world, your name is written. Then as you live, all that you do or say or think is written down. I'm talking *everything*. You're worried about Facebook and Big Brother invading your privacy? They've got nothing on these books.

Alongside these is another book that

> was opened, which is the Book of Life. And the dead were judged according to their works, by the things which were written in the books. The sea gave up the dead who were in it, and Death and Hades delivered up the dead who were in them. And they were judged, each one according to his

works. Then Death and Hades were cast into the lake of
fire. This is the second death. And anyone not found written in the Book of Life was cast into the lake of fire (Revelation 20:12-15).

There are the books of life and there is *the* Book of Life. This volume
was written with the blood of Jesus; therefore, it cannot be blotted out.
If your name is not found there, that's it. The lake of fire is your final
destination.

WHICH PLACE WILL YOU BE IN?

So, who goes where? In the Old Testament era, both the faithful
and the unfaithful went to Hades—the faithful to Abraham's bosom
(the good side) and the unfaithful to the place of torment. After the
cross, unbelievers continued to go to torment in Hades, but believers
began going directly into the presence of God. At the rapture, church-
age believers who have already died will lead the way into resurrection,
followed by believers who are still alive. The Old Testament saints will
be resurrected at the second coming, along with the tribulation martyrs. The rest of Hades will be resurrected to judgment at the end of the
millennium. Nonbelievers will be judged as unworthy and sent into
the lake of fire for eternity. Believers will find themselves celebrating
the arrival of the New Jerusalem in the new heavens and the new earth.

There is a place for everyone, and everyone will be in their place.
The question is, Which place will you be in? If you don't know for sure
that you have experienced your second birth, then you can't know with
certainty whether you will be part of the first resurrection. There is a
way, however, that you can know without a doubt. Paul wrote to the
church in Rome, "If you confess with your mouth the Lord Jesus and
believe in your heart that God has raised Him from the dead, you will
be saved. For with the heart one believes unto righteousness, and with
the mouth confession is made unto salvation" (Romans 10:9-10). All
this means is that if you truly believe that Jesus is who He has said He
is—the promised Messiah, God Himself—and you commit to Him

as your Lord, the one you will strive to follow all your life, you will be saved from the second death and the second resurrection. Your eternity will be secure. You will forever enjoy the company of the Creator God in His new heaven and new earth.

CHAPTER 12

A SINISTER STRATEGY

The Deceiver and the Deceived

Why?
Now that we have the parallel yet distinct histories and futures of Israel and the church sorted out—now that we have seen clearly God's choice of His two peoples, His purposes for His two peoples, and His plans for His two peoples—it's time we come to an uncomfortable yet necessary question. Why throughout history has there been such a concerted global effort to, at the least, marginalize the Jewish people, and at most, to eradicate them altogether? To answer this question, we need to revisit the one who is leading the effort to shift Israel from "chosen" status to "forgotten" or "forsaken."

Dwight L. Moody wrote, "The Bible will keep you from sin, or sin will keep you from the Bible."[12] That is such a simple yet profound statement. In essence, he is saying that the less you know about the things of God, the more you are ready to be deceived by the one who pretends to be God. Who is the one who pretends to be God? Satan. It wouldn't take more than a couple sessions on a couch with a good psychiatrist for the devil to be diagnosed with a massive and terminal god complex. In the book of Isaiah, God accuses Satan, saying,

You have said in your heart:
"I will ascend into heaven,
I will exalt my throne above the stars of God;
I will also sit on the mount of the congregation
On the farthest sides of the north;
I will ascend above the heights of the clouds,
I will be like the Most High" (14:13-14).

Satan wanted to be on par with God, but created can never equal Creator. As a result of his misplaced arrogance, he was cast out of heaven and condemned. Now he lives for two purposes: First, to somehow short-circuit God's plan, which, as we saw in Revelation, ends with him in the lake of fire. Second, if he is unable to escape his destiny, to take as many souls as he can with him into eternal punishment. His methodology for accomplishing both goals is the same—deceit.

In speaking of the devil, Jesus said, "He was a murderer from the beginning, and does not stand in the truth, because there is no truth in him. When he speaks a lie, he speaks from his own resources, for he is a liar and the father of it" (John 8:44). Satan is the father of lies, which makes sense. He is the opposite of all things God. So if Jesus is the Truth (John 14:6), then Satan is a liar. His plan is to deceive the world. And the primary target of his deceit is Israel. Why? First, because if he can destroy Israel, then God's ultimate plan for the nation's salvation cannot happen. And if God's plan is not carried out exactly as He has established, then God's Word is proven wrong. Truth suddenly becomes a lie. Second, Satan hates what God loves. Israel is dear to the Lord. As we saw in an earlier chapter, He refers to the nation as His beloved wife. If Satan can hurt what God loves, then he hurts God Himself.

SATAN'S STRATEGIES AGAINST ISRAEL

What does this plan to deceive the world with regard to Israel look like? Satan's strategies are very simple: First, he will make the nations want to get rid of Israel. Second, he will make Christians think that God is done with Israel. Third, he will make the Israelis tired of being persecuted so that they will forsake the things of God. These are very basic yet amazingly shrewd strategies, and Satan has been working on them steadily for thousands of years.

Make the Nations Want to Get Rid of Israel

Many times in the Bible, we see God using ungodly nations to punish Israel. Yet the minute those nations are done, He turns around and judges them. *Wait, God*, we think. *How is that fair? They were only doing what You wanted them to do.* Our confusion comes when we look only at the actions and not at the origins of the actions. These nations' rejection of God was not caused by the Almighty. He did not plant in them a spirit of rebellion or a desire for idol worship. These nations chose their path away from the truth all on their own.

In the same way, these nations' hatred toward Israel did not come from God, because God is love. To implant hatred would be to go against His character. If hatred is the opposite of love, then its source must be the opposite of God—the devil. He is the one who deceives people into allowing such animus for others in their hearts. God, who has the wisdom and power to take anything bad and use it for good, is able to use this sinful hatred to accomplish His will. This is part of God's brilliance. Just as Joseph said to his brothers, "As for you, you meant evil against me; but God meant it for good, in order to bring it about as it is this day, to save many people alive" (Genesis 50:20). That doesn't excuse the haters for their actions. Sin is still sin, and unatoned-for sin must always be punished.

We can see Satan deceiving the nations and God using that for His good all the way back to the time of the Egyptian pharaohs. They wanted to destroy the Jews by killing the male children, but God rescued them through His mighty works. Once the Hebrews fled Egypt, the Egyptians again wanted to wipe them out, but God opened up a path through the Red Sea—a path that subsequently closed on the Egyptian army and chariots, bringing judgment on the nation for its sins. Even as the Jewish people were on the road to the Promised Land, the nations came after them. The Amalekites and others all took their shot at accomplishing Satan's bidding.

Once the Israelites were in the Promised Land, the devil kept up his attacks. He used the Philistines, a people who originated in the Greek Isles. When drought and famine hit their land, they hopped on their boats and set off for a better location. This brought them first to Egypt, then to Gaza on the east coast of the Mediterranean. Eventually, they moved inland into Canaan—Israel.

At first the Philistines lived side by side with the Israelites. But then they started saying, "Hmmmm, this looks like a pretty easy opportunity here. We brought our iron with us, but these backward Israelites are still living in the Bronze Age." So the Philistines set about trying to take over. At one point, they sent out one of their heroes—a huge man with an enormous sword and spear—to taunt the Israelites. "You kill me, we belong to you. I kill you, you belong to us. Who will give it a shot?" There were no takers in the Israelite army, so it took one young man who just happened to be visiting his brothers to step up and say, "God and I will meet your challenge, tough guy." One smooth stone to the forehead later, the threat from the Philistines was gone.

After the Philistines, the Assyrians attacked and took away all of northern Israel. Then came the Babylonians, who destroyed Solomon's Temple and deported the rest of the Jews, sending them away to the exile. Next, following the Persians' permission for the Jews to return to Judea, Alexander the Great showed up. He came like a wrecking ball through all the lands, taking for himself everything he set his eye on. Part of his agenda was to promote the worship of the Greek gods, a goal his successors also took to heart. The worship of other gods would play well with those nations who were already polytheistic, but not so much with the Jews. When the people of Israel refused to bow before the Greek pantheon of gods, the Hellenistic army entered the Temple, desecrated it, slaughtered a pig on the altar, and attempted to force the Jews to bow down. This started a revolt that led to the Greeks being driven out of the country. The Jews then rededicated the Temple—an event that is remembered every year in the celebration of Hanukkah.

Stepping next into the empire vacuum was Rome. Initially, the Romans didn't want to get rid of the Jews. They just wanted land

and were fairly content to let the peoples they conquered do their own thing—as long as they paid their taxes and didn't rebel. But the Romans soon learned that the Jewish people were stiff-necked and didn't want to be ruled by anybody. In AD 70, the Romans came in and destroyed the Second Temple. Then, after a revolt in AD 135 led by Simon bar Kokhba, the emperor Hadrian leveled Jerusalem, chased out the remaining Jews, and renamed the land Syria Palaestina. Thus, the name *Palestine* was born.

Yet somehow, even after all these attempts by Satan and his proxies, the Jews remained alive. Years later, after the Jews had begun trickling back into Jerusalem, the Byzantines came. With them came a new tactic that would last for centuries, even into today. Rather than wiping out the Jews with invading armies, they began spreading lies about the Jews—hideous things that made anyone who heard the violent and bloody stories want to kill the Jews themselves. Now the persecution was not just governmental, but personal.

After the Byzantines came the cross. And who brought the cross? The Crusaders. You may not know this, but the cross is a big problem for the Jew. When he sees the cross, his mind is taken to a very bloody history. The Crusaders—primarily Christian Catholic knights from Western Europe—marched into the Middle East and beheaded thousands of Jews. Not only that, but they took whole Jewish communities, locked them into their synagogues, set the buildings on fire, and burned the people alive. It was said that in 1099, when the Crusaders arrived, the streets of Jerusalem flowed with rivers of blood. If there is one thing that Muslims and Jews share, it is a hatred of the Crusaders. These knights came in wearing the ultimate symbol of Christ's loving sacrifice, and they proceeded to do anything and everything that was antithetical to that perfect love.

The persecution didn't just stay in and around the Holy Land. In 1492, the same year that King Ferdinand and Queen Isabella sent Columbus out to sail the ocean blue, they also issued a proclamation to expel all the Jews from Spain. This banishment came after several years of severe persecution under the infamous Spanish Inquisition. Portugal followed suit four years later in 1496. Throughout Europe, occasional violent pogroms and persecutions would drive Jewish communities from one location to another.

At the beginning of the twentieth century, a new attack took place with the publication of *The Protocols of the Elders of Zion*. This completely fabricated book detailed the supposed secret plan of the Jews to take over the world and called on people to stop this sinister plot before it was too late. First published in Russia, *The Protocols* spread through Europe, leading to the massacre of many Jewish people. It even found its way into the United States, where Henry Ford, founder of the Ford Motor Company, financed the printing and distribution of half a million copies of this evil book of lies. It's amazing that one book could cause such terror and destruction. People's ears are always ready to hear the deceptive words of the devil.

In the midst of this anti-Semitic environment, an Austrian man rose to power in Germany. At first Adolf Hitler tried to encourage the Jews to leave German lands. But as he continued to expand the Third Reich, he kept finding more and more Jews across every new border. So he determined to get rid of them once and for all. In order to accomplish this Final Solution, he had to convince the Germans that the Jewish people were not actually people.

Imagine living in a nice gated community where all the neighbors get along. Next door to you lives a little boy who has a beautiful Persian cat that he adores. One day you are out in your yard, and you see the cat running toward the street. At the same time, a car is traveling down the road headed right for the cat. Would you help? Of course—even you dog lovers would do all you could to save the feline ball of fluff. Why? Because it is the right thing to do, and it will make the boy happy.

But what if your neighbor has been complaining that there is a big, nasty rat in his house that has been biting the family and sucking their blood and eating their food and spreading diseases? If you saw that rat heading for the street and a car coming directly toward it, would you step in to help? Of course not. In fact, you would probably encourage the driver to go faster.

This is exactly what Hitler did with the German people. Using movies and radio and print, he convinced them that the Jews were nothing but rats who were eating their food and sucking their blood and spreading diseases. If the Germans didn't get rid of the Jews, the Jews would surely wipe out the Germans. Through a constant barrage of propaganda, the humanity of the Jews was removed in the eyes of millions of people in the Third Reich. Once humanity was removed, concentration camps and gas chambers soon followed.

After World War II ended, the State of Israel was born in 1948. Immediately, five Arab armies came at Israel from all sides. And the attacks weren't just from the outside. Local Arabs rioted and killed Jews within Israel's borders too. But did this finish the Jewish people? Of course not. God once again protected His people, giving them a miraculous victory. Satan's strategy cannot and will not ever stop God's plan.

In 1973, on Yom Kippur—the Day of Atonement, the holiest day of the Jewish year—a coalition army led by Egypt and Syria opened a coordinated attack against Israel. It was a terrible mismatch, with the Arab armies mobilizing forces equivalent in size to that of NATO and Europe on Israel's border. There were 1,400 Syrian tanks on the northern front going up against Israel's paltry 100 tanks. On the southern border, Egypt brought 600,000 soldiers backed by 2,000 tanks and 550 aircraft. Israel had nearly nothing to stand in their way. All in all, the enemy forces had more than a million troops—that was equal to almost a third of the entire population of Israel at the time. Imagine it—that would be like the United States suddenly being invaded by an army of 110 million soldiers.

When the attack began, Israeli prime minister Golda Meir picked up the phone and placed a call to US President Richard Nixon. Even though it was 3:00 a.m., Nixon took the call. Meir told him, "Mr. President, if you are not going to help us, then Israel will not survive even twenty-four hours."

After a pause, the president replied, "Golda, every night when I was young, my mother used to read Bible stories to me at night. One evening, as she was reading, she paused and said, 'Richard, I want you to promise me that if you ever get to the point that you can save the lives of the Jewish people, that you won't ever hesitate to do so.' Then my mom went back to reading the story, and she never talked about it again. Now, with this phone call, I understand for the first time why I became the president of the United States." Nixon hung up the phone, and over the next twenty-four hours, the largest airlift of armaments since World War II took place. Every US military base in the Middle East was mobilized, and Israel survived the 1973 war.

Something in Nixon's mother, because of her being consumed by the Word of God, made her understand that the role of the Christian is to be on the side of Israel. Satan seeks to destroy; God seeks to preserve. The United States has been in the role of preserver with Israel for many years, and God has blessed America as a result. It all goes back to the Abrahamic covenant, when the Lord said He will bless those who bless Abraham's descendants and will curse those who don't. I believe that much of the success of Donald Trump's presidency is directly related to the way he has respected and supported Israel.

Later came the 1990–1991 Gulf War, when Saddam Hussein launched thirty-nine SCUD missiles into towns in Israel. The Iraqis especially targeted Tel Aviv—our most populated area. While property damage was caused by these tactical ballistic missiles, miraculously, only one life was lost—and that was from a heart attack.

Then the Palestinian uprising—the Intifada—took place. But it wasn't the violence that scared us most; it was the education. Palestinian children were and are being taught to hate the Jews using learning materials that are not very different than the old Nazi propaganda. Even while Israel is forced to kill terrorists, we do so with a complete awareness that in Gaza and the West Bank, the Palestinians are growing new generations of terrorists every day.

Even today there are regimes that vow to destroy the State of Israel. The enemy is consistent in his attempts to get rid of the Jewish people. No other nation has faced this kind of constant persecution for so long. This cannot be explained naturally; these are spiritual attacks we see taking place. Some people blame Islamists, but Muhammad wasn't around when the Amalekites came after Israel. The Muslims weren't there egging on pharaoh to kill all the male babies. Islam is just another weapon in the spiritual war chest in Satan's great struggle to deceive the nations into destroying that which God loves.

God has two peoples, and both are loved by Him
and have a bright future in His economy.

Make Christians Believe that God Is Done with Israel

Here is where we come to the saddest part of this book. This is where we see just how deeply many in the church have fallen prey to the deception of the enemy. My goal in this book has not been to take the arguments of Replacement Theology and debunk them one by one. In fact, my mission has not been to prove to you how wrong this belief system is, but to demonstrate through the Word of God just how impossible it is for Replacement Theology to be right. From Genesis to Revelation, we have seen God's plan for the nation of Israel. And from Matthew to Revelation—and even in many places in the Old Testament—we have seen God's plan for the church. God has two peoples, and both are loved by Him and have a bright future in His economy. That's why it is no surprise that the deceiver is so determined to create division and enmity between those whom God has chosen.

What happens when Satan attacks the body physically? It often becomes stronger and more united. This has been true throughout the church age, most recently in the persecution taking place in countries like China, Nigeria, and South Sudan. In the Western church, where there is little to no persecution, the enemy takes a different tack. Rather than attacking from the outside, he crawls in among us and tears us down from within. False teachings and false doctrines and false prophets weaken and divide the body. Rather than rooting ourselves in the Bible, we twist and compromise and explain away God's truth in order to make ourselves more palatable to the world.

A fundamental event took place in the Word of God when the Lord started something new with Abraham. He decided that He was going to bless the seed of Abraham, Isaac, and Jacob, and through them, deliver three amazing gifts: the belief in one God to the nations, the Word of God to the nations, and the Son of God to the nations. Not

surprisingly, Satan had a different idea. He had no interest in allowing the dissemination of a belief in one God, the creation of the Word
of God, and the incarnation of the Son of God for the good of the
nations. The problem was he couldn't stop God from carrying out His
plan. Again, when created goes up against Creator, created will lose
every time.

Because Satan couldn't halt God's plans, he decided to twist them.
He couldn't stop belief in one God. So he used his powers of deceit
to pervert people's views of that one God. For many, God became an
angry being whose only desire is to clobber people on the head when
they break one of His many invasive rules. For others, God morphed
into a big, cuddly teddy bear. He doesn't want to condemn anyone
or tell them that what they are doing is wrong. Rather, He's a giant,
needy hug-giver, ready to snuggle up with us whenever we decide to
give Him the time of day. Satan did the same with people's views of the
Son of God. He has twisted their perception of the true Christ, turning Him into someone whose only desire is for everyone to feel special
and accepted, and for you and me to walk around with a smile on our
face 24/7. If you're happy, then Jesus is happy.

This same twisting has taken place with the Word of God, particularly with regard to how Christians view the Jewish people. As we've
seen earlier, Replacement Theology says that God once chose Israel
to be "the apple of His eye" (Zechariah 2:8), but then Israel messed
up. The people rebelled, they worshipped idols, and worst of all, they
rejected the Messiah. Because of those egregious sins, God is no longer
interested in them. He condemned them, and now they are out of the
picture. And what of all the promises given to Israel throughout the
Old Testament? They belong to the church—the "new Israel."

This is not a new belief. Even back in the first-century church, Paul
could see this heresy coming. He sensed that all his teaching about how
we are no longer under the law but under grace could lead people to
believe that that's it—God is done with Israel. So, he addressed it very
clearly with no equivocation and pulling no punches. "I say then, has
God cast away His people? Certainly not! For I also am an Israelite, of
the seed of Abraham, of the tribe of Benjamin. God has not cast away

His people whom He foreknew" (Romans 11:1-2). Read that three or
four times. If you are a believer in Replacement Theology, read it seven
or eight times, until it is stuck in your brain. God is not fickle. He is
not capricious. He does not change His mind. He does not cast away
His people!

But Satan is a liar and the father of lies. He is good at what he does.
And ever since the beginning of the church, he has found those who
are ready to accept his deceptions.

Ignatius of Antioch, a late-first-century to early-second-century
theologian, taught that anyone who celebrated the Passover festival
aligned themselves with those who killed Jesus. In the second century,
Justin Martyr, another early church father, asserted that God's covenant
with the Jews was no longer binding and that the Gentiles had taken
their place. Around the same time, Irenaeus claimed that the Jews had
been disinherited from God's grace.

In the next century, Tertullian held the Jews responsible for Jesus'
death and said that, as a result, the Father rejected them. Then came
Origen, who was not only responsible for the allegorizing of much of
Scripture, but said that Jesus' crucifixion was all the fault of the Jews.
This led to a vicious anti-Semitic tone in his writings.

With time, the hatred and violence continued to progress.

The fourth century was very difficult for the Jews in relation to the
church. In 305, the Council of Elvira in Spain forbade Christians from
associating with Jewish people. This included everything from marry-
ing a Jew to sharing a meal with a Jew to simply blessing a Jew. Twenty
years later, at the Council of Nicea in Turkey, church leaders decided
to separate the celebration of Jesus' resurrection from the Jewish Feast
of First Fruits and, instead, align it with the pagan festival of Easter. To
justify this, they stated, "It was declared to be particularly unworthy for
this, the holiest of all festivals, to follow the custom of the Jews, who
had soiled their hands with the most fearful of crimes…And consequently, in unanimously adopting this mode, we desire, dearest brethren, to separate ourselves from the detestable company of the Jews…"[13]
Isn't it a wonder that Jews weren't pouring into the church in response
to the love of Jesus seen in His people?

Still in the fourth century, Eusebius looked at all the blessings and curses in Scripture, and boldly declared that the blessings belonged to the Gentiles and the curses to the Jews. John Chrysostom wrote, "The synagogue is not only a brothel and a theater, it is also a den of robbers and lodging place for wild beasts...They live for their bellies, they gape for the things of this world, their condition is not better than that of pigs or goats."[14] The Jews are just wild beasts, no better than pigs or goats? Wow, I'm guessing Chrysostom didn't get many bar mitzvah invitations.

I could keep going on, but I won't. Many who follow Replacement Theology look back and say, "See, even the church fathers believed that God has rejected the Jews. Who are you now to say that He hasn't?" It's because I don't look to the church fathers for my theology. They got many things right, and they got many things wrong. Besides, if you are going to throw Ignatius and Justin Martyr and Origen at me, I'll throw the apostle Paul back at you. How can someone possibly read Romans 9 and 11, and the consistent redemption themes directed to Israel throughout the prophets, and still say that God has forsaken those He called His own? God is 100 percent faithful to both His promises and His people. That truth is foundational to our faith.

Make the Israelis Tired of Being Persecuted

The third strategy Satan uses to deceive the world and make Israel irrelevant is to make the Israelis themselves tired of being persecuted. He wants to exhaust them. Wear them down. Make them so fed up with being at the tip of everyone else's spear that they'll do whatever it takes to become popular and get along with the rest of the world. Peace at any cost no matter what. And the strategy is working brilliantly. In fact, the Hebrew word *shalom*—which means "peace"—is the most common word found in Israeli songs. We are a people who are just tired of all the conflict and simply want to get along. If there was a Jewish national exclamation, it would be a heavy sigh.

It's not surprising to most that before 1948 came 1947. In that year prior to Israel's independence, the UN offered a plan for the division of the land between Arabs and Jews. This map was highly favorable toward the Arabs. They were given Jerusalem, the mountains of Judea and Samaria, the very strategic area of the Upper Galilee, and parts of the desert. It was a terrible deal for the Jewish people, but they were so exhausted after the Holocaust that they groaned, "Sure, we'll take it." Thank the Lord that the Arabs said, "No."

During the Six-Day War in 1967, Israeli troops made it all the way to the Temple Mount. They had taken Jerusalem back from the Jordanians and reunited the city. And they could have kept going. They could have gone up onto the Temple Mount and planted the Israeli flag. It was in their power to remove the Dome of the Rock and to raze the Al-Aqsa Mosque, and in their place to raise up the Third Temple. Yet they didn't. It was not time—the blowback would have been way too intense. Instead, the prime minister and defense minister left the Temple Mount in the hands of the Muslims, and they once again offered the Arabs a Palestinian state—which they, of course, rejected. Israel was willing to give up the most sacred place in all of Judaism because the people were too tired for another fight.

There's a picture from 1993 of the White House lawn in which Israeli prime minister Yitzhak Rabin is shaking hands with PLO chairman Yasser Arafat, all under the watchful, smiling eye of US President Bill Clinton. I like to call the picture "The Good, the Bad, and the Ugly," but I don't want to tell you who is who. This picture was taken to celebrate the signing of the Oslo Accords, which were supposed to bring peace to the Middle East. Did peace come? Of course not. In fact, all we got out of it was a T-shirt that said, "Our prime minister went to the White House and all he brought back was this lousy picture of him shaking hands with a man who is responsible for killing thousands of Jews." Not surprisingly, if that shirt actually did exist, it was likely not a huge seller. But just imagine: The leader of our nation shook hands with a murderer and terrorist whose primary goal in life was to drive the Jewish people into the Mediterranean Sea. That's how tired we are.

In 2004, after years of being brainwashed that Gaza and the West Bank belong to the Palestinians, we finally bought into the lie that if we would only evacuate those areas we would have peace. So Israel cleared out all the Jewish settlers and settlements from the Gaza Strip and bull-dozed the houses. We gave the land to the Palestinians free and clear. Why? Because we thought, *Peace! Finally!*

Do you know what the Palestinians did? Every settlement that was evacuated was replaced with a terrorist camp. And now—even to today—many missiles fly from Gaza into Israel. They are their free gifts to us. It's how they show their appreciation. You would think we would learn, but we're just too tired.

In June 2006, Israeli Defense Forces (IDF) corporal Gilad Shalit was kidnapped by Palestinian commandos on a raid into Israeli territory. For the next 1,934 days, he was held in a Hamas dungeon in Gaza while the IDF tried to rescue him and the government tried to negotiate his release. Finally, a deal was struck, and in exchange for this one corporal, Israel released back to Hamas 1,027 prisoners—many of them terrorists who had Jewish blood on their hands. That's how tired we are of conflict. I remember being very moved as I watched the helicopter carrying Shalit home fly right above my house. The whole nation was in tears. This was an insane deal—1,027 for 1. But we're so tired of any of our people suffering that we'll do whatever it takes to achieve peace.

This is the attitude that will prime Israel to accept the overtures of the Antichrist. When he comes with his message of *shalom*, the Jewish nation will be eagerly ready to receive him because all we want is to be loved and accepted. Our commitment to God's call to stand separate—to be holy—is long gone. Now our desire is to be one of the gang.

Satan's strategies are simple, and they are working very well.

ISRAEL AND THE CHURCH

Why is there so much enmity between the nations and Israel? And why—in the past and even into today—have so many in the church had a disdain for God's first chosen people? The answer to the *why* is directed to a *who*. The enemy wants to ensure that the Jews are viewed as forsaken and forgotten by God. Again, sadly, there are far too many in the church who are quick to buy into his lies.

*It is also our duty to protect the truth of Scripture
within the church from the deceptive doctrines
that remove the Jews from heart of the Creator.*

In the same way that the church has been eternally chosen by God to be His people, so have the Jews been chosen. We in the church need to recognize that truth. It is our responsibility to let the nations know that Israel is loved by God. It is also our duty to protect the truth of Scripture within the church from the deceptive doctrines that remove the Jews from the heart of the Creator. Finally, it is both our delight and our challenge to find ways to comfort Israel.

In Isaiah, we read, "'Comfort, yes, comfort My people!' says your God. 'Speak comfort to Jerusalem, and cry out to her'" (40:1-2). In the original Hebrew text, the word "comfort" is in the imperative case. In other words, it is a command. So God is commanding someone to comfort His people. For years I wondered, *To whom was God giving this command?* Then I came across 2 Corinthians 1, and it all became clear to me. Paul wrote, "Blessed be the God and Father of our Lord Jesus Christ, the Father of mercies and God of all comfort, who comforts us in all our tribulation, that we may be able to comfort those who are in any trouble, with the comfort with which we ourselves are comforted by God" (verses 3-4). There is only one group of people on planet Earth that has been given the ability to give comfort, including to Israel: the believers who comprise the church. This is our job. This is our joy.

What does that comfort look like? This is what we will explore in our final chapter.

CHAPTER 13

THE BLESSINGS
OF THE BLESSERS

How Can the Church Support Israel?

Clip-clop. Clip-clop. The man struggled to raise his cheek from the gritty ground as he sought to hone in on the sound. The simple head lift was no easy feat. The knots on the back of his skull from where the club had connected felt like hundred-pound weights pushing his face downward. Groaning, he forced a shift of perspective, giving his bleary, swollen eyes a glimpse of a man on a donkey. But this was no ordinary man—his fine traveling clothes and obviously well-bred beast of burden made it very clear that he was one of the set-apart ones. This passerby was a priest, a servant of the Temple. Relief flooded over the man. If there was anyone who might help him, it would certainly be this man of God. All his fears of being left out in the open overnight, exposed to the elements and the wild animals, were swept away. Tears came to his already-wet eyes.

"Help," he managed to cough out. "Please help."

But the priest didn't stop. He didn't even turn to look. The sprawled man knew there was no way he couldn't be seen. He was right on the side of the narrow road where the violent thieves had left him.

"Help me," he gasped. "Please don't leave me."

But soon the *clip-clop* faded, replaced by a tomb-like silence. The man's world faded back to darkness.

Pain shot through his side. He cried out and involuntarily pulled away. Looking up, he saw a man jumping backward with a walking stick in his hand. As surprised as he was to be awakened this way, this visitor seemed equally surprised to see the sprawled man was alive. Quickly putting two and two together, he realized that the visitor had just prodded him for signs of life by poking what must have been a broken rib or two. But despite the pain, relief filled him. Once again, this wasn't just any man—his tribal clothing and gear was that of a Levite. Maybe he didn't work in the Temple, but he was still a man of God. The stranded man was saved.

Then the Levite began backing away. On his face was a look of revulsion and fear and disgust. He continued his retreat all the way to the other side of the road, where he turned and hurried on his way toward Jericho. Hopelessness and helplessness overtook the man, and sobs wracked and twisted his damaged body.

More time passed, and this innocent victim knew that behind him, on the other side of the hills, the sun would soon be going down. What might happen then made him shudder. He began praying and soon lost consciousness once again.

A gentle hand shook his shoulder. He smiled, imagining it was his wife rousing him on one of those rare mornings when he was able to sleep past sunrise. Then the pain hit, and he snapped alert. He opened his eyes, and terror filled him. One look at the guy leaning over him, and the man had no doubt that he was about to be robbed again— maybe beaten, maybe killed. Staring down at him with a look of what had to be false concern was a Samaritan.

"Calm down, calm down," the Samaritan insisted as the wounded man tried to pull back.

"Get your hands off me! I have nothing left! They took it all—I swear!"

"Relax, my friend. I'm here to help," the other man said with a smile of compassion. "I have some balm in my bag that will help. Then let me get you on my donkey and down to Jericho. You'll not survive the night out here on your own."

It took only a moment for the wounded man to weigh his options and realize he had only one. Reluctantly at first, he let the Samaritan begin applying the medicinal ointment and wrapping his wounds. Soon his reticence turned to gratefulness, and he began thanking the foreigner over and over. It was a long and painful ride to Jericho, but eventually the man found himself in a bed at an inn and being tended to by a proper doctor.

THE CHURCH'S RESPONSIBILITY

When Jesus told this story, His point was that we should sacrificially love all people no matter who they are. As we read it, our focus is typically centered on the Good Samaritan and the fact that he did the right thing. We tend to spend much less time on the priest and the Levite who failed to do what they should have done. It wasn't that they were ignorant of what was right and what was wrong. The morality of helping versus not helping wouldn't have been in question for these men steeped in the law. They knew exactly what they should do, but simply chose not to do it. In the letter written by Jesus' brother, James, we read, "To him who knows to do good and does not do it, to him it is sin" (4:17). In other words, the sins of omission are just as sinful as the sins of commission. The priest and the Levite knew the right thing to do, so by not doing it, they sinned.

Therefore, if God has made it clear that the church has a responsibility to support Israel, yet Christians have turned their back on the Jewish people, then what conclusion must we come to? Again, sins of omission are still sins. The foundational question is this: Does the church have a responsibility today to the Jews?

Throughout this book, I've presented the biblical case that Israel is without a doubt a nation that the Lord has chosen for a reason and for a season. But the deception regarding Israel is prevalent across America and around the world and can be traced all the way back to the original sin of Genesis 3. From the moment Satan's fate was sealed, he has had it out for Israel. His influence is still great today.

Each day I get many hundreds of text messages, Facebook messages, and YouTube comments. You would be surprised at how many are laced with vulgar obscenities. Each day when I get up, I peruse these lovely "good morning" wishes. Not long ago I received a message from a man who purported to be a Christian. His loving suggestion was that since Israel was the source of most of the world's problems, the United States should just nuke our little nation—problem solved! And he is just one of so many with a virulent hatred of Israel.

Somewhere along the line, the lie has taken hold in the church that Israel today is somehow different than the Israel of the Old Testament. While the Israel of the Bible is something to be revered, the Israel of today can be fought against and boycotted and trashed. The assumption is that back then, Israel contained God's chosen people. But today, Israel is no different than any other nation filled with atheists and followers of a false religion.

A number of years ago, a prominent American theologian with an enormous following preached a sermon about Israel's place in God's economy. He said, "The promises made to Abraham, including the promise of the Land, will be inherited as an everlasting gift only by true, spiritual Israel, not disobedient, unbelieving Israel…By faith in Jesus Christ, the Jewish Messiah, Gentiles become heirs of the promise of Abraham, including the promise of the Land…Therefore, the secular state of Israel today may not claim a present divine right to the Land, but they and we should seek a peaceful settlement not based on present divine rights, but on international principles of justice, mercy, and practical feasibility."[15]

This is absolute baloney—not even the good kind you get from a proper Jewish deli. This is the root of the problem. When you take away Israel's divine rights and divine calling and godly destination, and instead you insert today's language of the "international principles of justice, mercy, and practical feasibility," God's Word is replaced by the world's mores. And what are our global society's morals of justice and mercy? It's for babies to not be born. It's for homosexuality and gender confusion to be celebrated. Every day the world's standards of justice and mercy are slipping further and further away from the Word of God. As Paul wrote, "Let God be true but every man a liar" (Romans 3:4).

We must use the Word of God as our one and only standard no matter how much it might go against our culture's definition of righteousness. And we must take the words of Scripture at face value even if they don't fit our preconceived doctrinal notions.

God wrote the Bible to be understood by men and women from the wisest to the simplest. That is why, as much as possible, we should use a straightforward, literal hermeneutic to understand the Scriptures. What you read in the Bible almost always means exactly what it seems to mean. You don't need a PhD in biblical studies to be able to discern the truth behind Moses' histories and David's psalms and Solomon's wisdom and Isaiah's prophecies and John's narratives and Paul's doctrine. Of course, we can get better understanding of various parts of Scripture the more we learn of the writings' historical and cultural contexts. But discovering cultural context will not suddenly open up some secret meaning or biblical code or allegorical interpretation. Sadly, this desire to find deeper meanings through allegorizing Scripture first started centuries ago with Origen and can still be found in the hermeneutics of those like the pastor mentioned earlier. This is essentially the hermeneutic of "While it may look pretty obvious that this is what the Bible says, who are you going to believe—me or your own lying eyes?"

TWO CHOSEN PEOPLES

God could not have made it any clearer that He is not One who abandons those who are His. The prophet Samuel declared, "The Lord will not forsake His people, for His great name's sake, because it has pleased the Lord to make you His people" (1 Samuel 12:22). Where is the room for the "Yeah, but…" in that statement? Even in Samuel's warning statement at the end of that particular speech, the threat of punishment for wickedness extends to that generation and its king—not to the Jewish people as a whole.

"But, Amir, that was a different time. It was before the Jews rejected the Messiah." True. However, as we've seen numerous times already, Paul lets us know that absolutely nothing has changed between God and Israel. "I say then, has God cast away His people? Certainly not! For I also am an Israelite, of the seed of Abraham, of the tribe of Benjamin. God has not cast away His people whom He foreknew" (Romans 11:1-2). It takes a very dexterous game of doctrinal Twister to "right hand blue, left foot green" away this bold, straightforward pronouncement.

God has used Israel to announce Himself to the Gentile world, and He is using the church to draw Israel back to Himself.

The Jews are God's chosen people. The church is God's chosen people. Why must so many insist that there only be one? Currently, only the latter of these two peoples are following the path of righteousness. But, honestly, that's nothing new for Israel. When in Israel's history have the Jews ever been all-in for God? Certainly not when they were wandering in the wilderness. Not during the time of the judges or even in the days of the kings. Remember when David made his escape from King Saul? His wife, Michal, took an idol that just happened to be in the house and placed it in David's bed with some goat's hair to fool King Saul's guards.

Even when the people of Israel came back from exile, they traded one false belief system for another—leaving behind their worship of idols they commenced to worship the law. If after Israel's history of rebellion and apathy toward God He never abandoned them, why would we think that a rebellious and apathetic modern Israel is any different? And if God has not abandoned Israel, why we would we as followers of God conclude we could treat the Jewish people with anything but love?

While we have emphasized the distinction between Israel and the church throughout this book, we must also recognize our interconnectedness. God has used Israel to announce Himself to the Gentile world, and He is using the church to draw Israel back to Himself.

Concerning the gospel they are enemies for your sake, but concerning the election they are beloved for the sake of the fathers. For the gifts and the calling of God are irrevocable. For as you were once disobedient to God, yet have now obtained mercy through their disobedience, even so these also have now been disobedient, that through the mercy shown you they also may obtain mercy. For God has committed them all to disobedience, that He might have mercy on all (Romans 11:28-32).

Yes, Israel is an unbelieving nation. But this is all part of God's plan. God's national irrevocable calling to the Jews sets the groundwork for His spiritual irrevocable calling to the church. His unfailing love for the Jewish people despite their sin and failings is what gives us confidence that His love will never fail us despite our own sin and failings. This interconnectedness goes both ways. It is God's mercy to the church—even through our disobedience—that shows law-centered Israel that His mercy is greater than their sins. If "God demonstrates His own love toward us, in that while we were still sinners, Christ died for us" (Romans 5:8), then how can we as God's people do anything less than sacrificially love the people of Israel while they are still in their sins?

God's unfailing love for the Jewish people despite their sin and failings is what gives us confidence that His love will never fail us despite our own sin and failings.

Let God be true and every man a liar—He will never abandon those whom He has called His own. Our responsibility as believers is to love that which God loves. God still loves His original chosen people. Those in the church who reject Israel must beware. If we find ourselves against or hating that which God loves, it will not be long before we start loving that which God is against or hates.

WHAT THE CHURCH SHOULDN'T DO

The church has been called to love and support Israel. However, there are those who take their Israel-love a little too far. First, there are some who, in their desire to see all Israel saved now rather than at the end of the tribulation, have thrown the Jewish people a spiritual lifeline. They have come up with the concept of a dual covenant—one for the Gentiles and one for the Jews. For the Gentiles of the new covenant, salvation is by grace "through faith, and that not of yourselves; it is the gift of God, not of works, lest anyone should boast" (Ephesians 2:8-9). But for the Jews who have rejected Christ and thus the grace that comes from His work on the cross, God in His love for His people allows them salvation through obedience to the old covenant law.

But Jesus Himself negated any possibility of the dual covenant view one night when a Pharisee made a clandestine visit to Him. In a statement that blew any chance of salvation by personal merit out the window, Jesus told this Jewish religious leader,

> Most assuredly, I say to you, unless one is born again, he cannot see the kingdom of God…And as Moses lifted up the serpent in the wilderness, even so must the Son of Man be lifted up, that whoever believes in Him should not perish but have eternal life. For God so loved the world that He gave His only begotten Son, that whoever believes in Him should not perish but have everlasting life (John 3:3,14-16).

There are no caveats. There are no distinctions between Jew and Gentile. The words "one" and "whoever" are all-inclusive. Salvation comes only through faith in Jesus Christ.

The second way people improperly love and support Israel is by falling into the trap of "imitation is the sincerest form of flattery." So many Gentiles say they want to become Jews. And, let me tell you, they can become pretty militant in their pseudo-Jewishness. I've had people become very unhappy with me when they look at my breakfast plate and see strips of a certain glorious pork product lined up alongside my eggs. "How could you, Amir? You're a Jew!" I tell them that if they want to start following Jewish dietary laws, go right ahead. Just leave my breakfast alone!

The Bible does not show us even one single case either in the Old or New Testament in which a person is saved by keeping the law. In fact, the Bible makes it clear that no one can perfectly keep the law. And because the law is holy in its entirety, if you break one law, you break them all. There is only one who has fulfilled the law, and that's Jesus. God didn't give us the law so that we could complete the law. The law was given so that we would understand that we need a Savior—that we can't deal with our sin on our own.

Still, what do some people do? They suggest that Gentiles should start keeping the law and all the festivals. Sure, salvation comes by grace through faith, but then you also need to do this and you need to do that. They promote a Jesus-plus doctrine of salvation. These people are getting Romans 11 completely backward. Paul wrote, "Through [the Jews'] fall, to provoke them to jealousy, salvation has come to the Gentiles" (Romans 11:11). For many Christians, rather than letting their salvation by grace provoke the Jews to jealousy, they are letting the Jews' adherence to the law provoke themselves to jealousy.

WHAT THE CHURCH SHOULD DO

If those are the *don'ts*, then what are the *dos*? How should the church support their fellow chosen people of God?

Pray

First and foremost, the church must be praying for Israel. There are three prayers believers should be offering for the Jewish nation. The first two are found in Psalm 122: "Pray for the peace of Jerusalem: 'May they prosper who love you. Peace be within your walls, prosperity within your palaces'" (verses 6-7). First, pray for peace. For all the negative happenings in 2020, it was a banner year for Israel's peace with the

Arab world. As of the time of this writing, with the help of the United States, Israel has normalized relations with the United Arab Emirates, Bahrain, Sudan, and Morocco. And, by all indications, Saudi Arabia will be next. God is listening to the prayers of His church.

The second prayer we find in that passage is for Israel's prosperity. When we look at Israel now compared to when it declared independence seventy-two years ago, it is impossible to miss the hand of God at work. Israel is a world leader in energy, technology, agriculture, medicine, and so many other areas. Never before in the history of the world has a nation blossomed so rapidly, particularly in the midst of constant international opposition. This can only be the work of a God who holds Israel as "the apple of His eye" (Deuteronomy 32:10).

We can also see in this psalm the retroactive nature of support for Israel. As we love the nation and desire peace and prosperity for it, we, too, will prosper. I believe that from the moment President Truman recognized the newly declared nation of Israel in 1948, America has been the biggest recipient of this promise.

Our third prayer for the Jewish people is for their salvation. Yes, there will be a national revival at the end of the tribulation. But in the meantime, we must be praying that God rescues more and more Jews from having to endure Jacob's trouble by saving them now through faith in the forgiveness that is found in the blood of Christ shed on the cross. I am one of those Jews who did not have to wait to be able to recognize the One whom I pierced. I have experienced the freedom that comes from putting my works behind me and trusting instead in the work of my Savior. Even as we wait for that final revival, let us pray for revival now in the nation of Israel.

Proclaim

The second way churches can support Israel is to preach the truth about God's continued love for the Jewish people. We've already talked about misguided pastors who teach that God has rejected Israel. However, there is another group of pastors that contribute to the biblical ignorance of their flock—those who don't preach about Israel at

all. Like that embarrassing, ill-mannered uncle whom nobody likes
to invite to Christmas dinner, modern Israel has become persona non
grata in many of today's churches. By ignoring Israel, we miss an ideal
opportunity to teach the long-suffering love of God, the bottomless
well of His forgiveness, and the peace-giving assurance of our salvation.
Pastors, do not neglect Israel. Celebrate the nation as the demonstration of the power of God that it is. Let your people see, through Israel,
that God is still a miracle-working God.

Give

A final way to show love for Israel is to financially support the Jewish people. "Now, wait a second, Amir. I don't remember reading that
in the Bible." Well, it's there—I'm not making it up. As Paul was wrapping up his letter to the church in Rome, he encouraged the believers
there to give to the Jewish church in Jerusalem. "I am going to Jerusalem to minister to the saints. For it pleased those from Macedonia and
Achaia to make a certain contribution for the poor among the saints
who are in Jerusalem. It pleased them indeed, and they are their debtors.
For if the Gentiles have been partakers of their spiritual things, their
duty is also to minister to them in material things" (Romans 15:25-27).
Using the churches of Macedonia and Achaia (Philippi, Thessalonica,
Berea, and Corinth) as examples, Paul challenged the Roman Christians to financially support their Jewish brothers and sisters. Why?
Because they owed them. From the Jews, the Gentiles received "spiritual things." It is only fair that, in return, the Gentiles bless the Jews
with "material things." We who are believers are also recipients of these
"spiritual things," as outlined in the last chapter. Why would we think
that we are any different than the Romans?

Now, I'm not saying that you should get out your checkbook
and write a $50 check to the State of Israel. While I'm sure Israel's
minister of finance would be appreciative, our nation can probably
survive without your sacrifice. This is also not my plea for you to support Behold Israel. If God leads you that direction, then praise the
Lord; He is good. However, there are many other missionaries and

ministries that are also directly ministering to the needs of the Jewish people.

I have a pastor friend who is fond of telling his congregation, "If, in your prayer time, you feel God calling you to another church, I am perfectly fine with that. I don't care what church you are serving in as long as you are serving in God's church." I feel the same way when it comes to believers supporting the Jewish people.

How do you find a ministry to support?

Pray. That's the most important step you can take.

Do your homework. There are a lot of shady ministries out there.

Find a ministry that directly blesses God's chosen people. It may support the physically needy, the materially needy, or the spiritually needy—God can work through them all. Remember, many unbelievers need to see the love of Christ before they are ready to hear about the love of Christ.

Give. Pray and listen to God. He will make clear what He is calling you to do.

Unbelievers need to see the love of Christ before
they are ready to hear about the love of Christ.

A MARVELOUS PROMISE

God will never leave nor forsake that which is His own. As a Jew, I receive great comfort from knowing that He has not forgotten my people, and that in the end, He will draw them to Himself. And, as a believing member of God's church, I derive great comfort from knowing that the same God who will not abandon Israel will not abandon me—no matter what my faults or failures may be. Instead, all of us— Jew and Gentile, Israel and the church—may hold to the marvelous promise given to Israel when the people had hit rock bottom:

Through the LORD's mercies we are not consumed,
Because His compassions fail not.
They are new every morning;
Great is Your faithfulness (Lamentations 3:22-23).

NOTES

1. "Facts & Stats," *International Overdose Awareness Day*, April 13, 2020, www.overdoseday.com/facts-stats/.

2. "Opioid Data Analysis and Resources," *Centers for Disease Control and Prevention*, March 19, 2020, www.cdc.gov/drugoverdose/data/analysis.html.

3. "Opioid Data Analysis and Resources."

4. "Opioid Data Analysis and Resources."

5. "Walter Rothschild and the Balfour Declaration," *Contact Us FAQs: The Rothschild Archive*, www.rothschildarchive.org/contact/faqs/walter_rothschild_and_the_balfour_declaration.

6. "Pre-State Israel," *The San Remo Conference*, www.jewishvirtuallibrary.org/the-san-remo-conference.

7. Jonathan Lipnick, "To the Place of Trumpeting," *Biblical Hebrew and Holy Land Studies Blog—IIBS.com*, July 18, 2018, www.https://blog.israelbiblicalstudies.com/holy-land-studies/to-the-place-of-trumpeting/.

8. "Current World Population," *Worldometer*, accessed October 30, 2020, https://www.worldometers.info/world-population/.

9. Loup Besmond de Senneville, "Dans Le Monde, Un Chrétien Sur Quatre Est Évangélique," *La Croix*, January 25, 2016, https://www.la-croix.com/Religion/Monde/Dans-monde-chretien-quatre-evangelique-2016-01-25-1200735150.

10. Oscar Schwartz, "The Rise of Microchipping: Are We Ready for Technology to Get under the Skin?," *The Guardian*, November 8, 2019, https://www.theguardian.com/technology/2019/nov/08/the-rise-of-microchipping-are-we-ready-for-technology-to-get-under-the-skin.

11. The Churchill Society London, *Churchill's Speeches*, accessed October 30, 2020, http://www.churchill-society-london.org.uk/EndoBegn.html.

12. D.L. Moody, as cited by J.H. Carstens, "The Greatness of the Bible," *The Standard*, June 18, 1910, 7.

13. "Council of Nicea I: Text - IntraText CT," *intratext.com*, accessed October 31, 2020, http://www.intratext.com/IXT/ENG0425/_PY.HTM.

14. Roger Pearse, "John Chrysostom, Against the Jews, Homily 1," *Tertullian.org*, accessed October 31, 2020, http://www.tertullian.org/fathers/chrysostom_adversus_judaeos_01_homily1.htm.

15. John Piper, "Israel, Palestine and the Middle East," *Desiring God*, March 7, 2004, https://www.desiringgod.org/messages/israel-palestine-and-the-middle-east.

Israel and the Church Study Guide

To fully grasp what God has in store for the future, it's vital to understand His promises to Israel. The *Israel and the Church Study Guide* will help you do exactly that, equipping you to explore the Bible's many revelations about what is yet to come.

The Day Approaching

As a native Israeli of Jewish roots, Amir Tsarfati provides a distinct perspective that weaves biblical history, current events, and Bible prophecy together to shine light on the mysteries about the end times. In *The Day Approaching*, he points to the scriptural evidence that the return of the Lord is imminent.

The Day Approaching Study Guide

Jesus Himself revealed the signs that will alert us to the nearness of His return. In *The Day Approaching Study Guide*, you'll have the opportunity to take an up-close look at what those signs are, as well as God's overarching plans for the future, and how those plans affect you today.

To learn more about Harvest House books and
to read sample chapters, visit our website:

www.harvesthousepublishers.com

HARVEST HOUSE PUBLISHERS
EUGENE, OREGON